FERNS

& FERN ALLIES

OF THE SMOKIES

WRITTEN BY
MURRAY EVANS

GREAT SMOKY MOUNTAINS
ASSOCIATION
Gatlinburg, Tennessee

EDITED BY: Steve Kemp
SERIES DESIGN BY: Christina Watkins
PRODUCTION BY: Lisa Horstman
EDITORIAL REVIEW & ASSISTANCE BY: Coralie Bloom, Kent Cave,
Patricia Cox, Elise LeQuire, Janet Rock
COVER PHOTOGRAPH BY: Adam Jones

PRINTED IN HONG KONG

1 2 3 4 5 6 7 8 9

ISBN 0-937207-45-4

Great Smoky Mountains Association is a nonprofit organization
which supports the educational, scientific, and historical programs of
Great Smoky Mountains National Park. Our publications are an educational service intended to enhance the public's understanding and
enjoyment of the national park. If you would like to know more
about our publications, memberships, and projects, please contact:
Great Smoky Mountains Association, 115 Park Headquarters Road,
Gatlinburg, TN 37738 (865) 436-7318. www.SmokiesStore.org

This book is dedicated to the hardy band of pteridologists who search the globe to study ferns in their natural habitats and on their own terms.

CONTENTS

INTRODUCTION

This little book on the ferns and fern allies of Great Smoky Mountains National Park is intended to not only help you identify these interesting plants, but also to arouse your curiosity to learn more about them. For lots of folks, "they all look alike." I got started with ferns in 1956 when I went to Taiwan to teach English for two years, which led to a graduate degree in the ecology of ferns of Taiwan. I am still learning.

There are not a lot of species in the park—about 64 counting some pretty esoteric and hard to find examples. The species identification section also includes other ferns which are known from the neighborhood of the park, but have just not yet been found within it. The ferns in the park comprise a nice group of plants to identify and to learn something of their biology and natural history. When you have gotten some of these species under control, then move further out and keep looking. You will find many more on either side of the park in Tennessee and North Carolina, more yet in the southeastern U. S., and many more in Central America and the West Indies. My hope is that the material presented here will not be an end in itself, but the beginning of understanding a wonderful group of plants.

THINGS TO LOOK FOR IN FERNS . . . .

Ferns are a bit unusual, and, in order to learn to identify them, we have to learn a few new tricks as to what to look for.

Ferns (Pteridophytes) are "vascular plants" as are Angiosperms (flowering plants) and Gymnosperms (pines, hemlocks, cedars, spruce, and the like), so they develop specialized cells organized into **vascular bundles** in the stems and leaves. These bundles or veins move water and nutrients through the plant. Mosses, liverworts, algae and fungi are considered "non-vascular plants" although some of them have bands of cells that move materials from cell to cell with some increase in efficiency, but not with the efficiency of the tissue systems in vascular plants.

Ferns are all herbaceous plants; they do not have the woody stems and branches as in trees and shrubs. Therefore they generally do not get very big. Tropical tree ferns do become really tall, but they do not do so by laying down wood layer by layer, year by year. They grow tall by a complicated interlacing of tough vascular bundles and fiber bundles similar to a woven rope. This provides enough strength to hold up these stems so that they may grow to 15 or 20 feet tall, but they are basically just a **rhizome** like those of "ordinary" ferns.

There are also a lot of ferns, again mostly in warmer climates, that look huge, but what you are seeing are large leaves growing 10 or 15 feet long. None of these occur in the Smokies; the longest fern leaves in our flora might grow to about four feet tall, unless you count the Climbing Fern (*Lygodium palmatum*) in which the leaf climbs other vegetation like a delicate vine.

Ferns and fern allies do not produce seeds, so there are no seed pods or cones for distinguishing characteristics. The cones, or strobili, in the fern allies contain spores, not seeds, so although they may look like tiny spruce or pine cones, they really are a different stage of the reproductive life cycle (see "The Fern Life Cycle").

What ferns and fern allies do produce are **sporangia** in various arrangements and positions, usually on the underside or the edge of the leaves. The fern allies produce cones (**strobili**) with just one sporangium per leaf (cone scale, or **sporophyll**) at the base of the upper side of the leaf. The ferns usually aggregate several to many sporangia in a special cluster called a **sorus** (plural sori). There may be accessory structures with the sporangia, like hairs or glands among the sporangia, or club-like **sporangiasters**. Frequently there is a flap of tissue (an **indusium**) over the cluster of young sporangia, which usually shrivels up and is pushed aside as the sporangia enlarge and mature. These are presumed to function as protection for the tender developing sporangia and spores, and dry up when the sporangia mature and release the spores. The placement of the sori on the leaf, and the shape of the sorus and indusium (round, elongated, hooked, horse-shoe shaped, etc.) all are helpful identification characteristics.

Hairs, scales, and glands are also important identifying characteristics. Hairs are elongated strings of cells only one cell wide but many cells long; scales are two-dimensional, many cells long and wide; glands are bulbous cells; if on the tip of a short hair, then a "glandular hair."

In the absence of fancy colorful flowers, big scaly cones, or enormous variation in size and shape that appear in flowering plants and gymnosperms, these rather technical and subtle characteristics are what make identification of ferns and fern allies fun, and challenging.

A final caveat, or two. Use a hand lens, 10X is preferable, and learn how to hold it steady between your face and your specimen using your fingers to connect all three. Practice! If you really get taken with all this, a dissecting scope at home with a range of optics from 10X to 45X or 60X and a fixed light will really put you in business. Collecting plants or plant parts (other than berries and mushrooms) is prohibited in the national park.

And finally, don't work with immature plants. If you can't find the sori or strobili, or they don't look nearly mature (they turn golden, brownish, or blackish as the spores mature in the sporangia) then look for better specimens. You need to know what the mature plants look like before you try to identify immature ones.

THE FERN LIFE CYCLE . . . .

Nearly all plants and animals reproduce sexually through variations of a standard sexual life cycle. In plants, the fertilized egg develops into an embryo, and ultimately into an adult plant. In seed plants (flowering plants and gymnosperms) this embryo development occurs in seeds either within flowers or on the gymnosperm cones. When the seed is put into appropriate environmental conditions, it will germinate and grow into an adult plant. The seed is a complex structure of many cells in specialized organs which may be packed into something as small as a nearly microscopic orchid seed, or as huge as a coconut.

Pteridophytes (ferns and fern allies) do not produce seeds. Instead, their dormant stage, or stopping point in the life cycle, is the spore. The spore is only one cell, and in nearly all cases is microscopically small, and is coated with a tough and often highly ornamented spore coat. This helps protect spores so they may live several months to a few years under ideal conditions. Spores are produced in sporangia on sporophyte plants (literally "spore plants"). When we are enjoying ferns and fern allies, these are the plants we are looking at, and we can see the sporangium clusters (sori) or strobili on the appropriate leaf parts.

Spores are usually dispersed by wind, but in a few cases they may disperse by water or even animals. They are usually released by the mechanical opening of the sporangia. A special group of cells (annuli) may actually catapult the spores out into the air. Upon landing in suitable growing conditions, they will germinate and grow, not into the familiar leafy plant from whence they came, but into a flat, more or less heart-shaped, green plant (the gametophyte), one cell thick and less than ¼" across.

Rhizoids, root-like extensions of some of the cells, anchor this plant to its substrate. Sex organs are borne on the underside. Antheridia (male), looking like microscopic soccer balls and containing swimming sperm, are borne among the rhizoids. Archegonia (female), looking like microscopic short chimneys and each containing a single egg, develop near the notch, or indentation, on the gametophyte margin.

Although most Pteridophyte gametophytes are bisexual, self fertilization is usually suppressed through chemical inhibitors, or differing timing of sex organ maturation. When released, the sperm swim through a film of water (rain, dew, etc.) to fertilize the egg, the first step in the production of the new sporophyte plant. This fertilized egg now contains the chromosome sets (and genes) from both the sperm and the egg; pairs, rather than half of each pair. This fertilized egg grows, divides, becomes an embryo, and then an immature leafy sporophyte plant, which overgrows and destroys the gametophyte plant on which it began. Eventually, perhaps over several years, it becomes mature. It produces sporophylls with sporangia containing spores, which completes the recurring cycle.

This is the Pteridophyte life cycle, with free-living, independent sporophyte and gametophyte generations. This unites the ferns and the fern allies into a coherent group, and sets them apart from the flowering plants and gymnosperms.

As in much of the natural world, there are exceptions. Not all new Pteridophyte plants arise through sexual reproduction and alternation of independent gametophyte and sporophyte generations. The Walking Fern (*Asplenium rhizophyllum*) produces plantlets at the tips of leaves, which become, over time, new independent adult plants. The bulblets of the Bulblet Bladder Fern (*Cystopteris bulbifera*) drop off the sporophyte plant and grow into new sporophyte plants. Even more commonly, the rhizomes of most ferns, either by divisions of the compact crown or by forking of the creeping rhizomes produce new plants. If the intervening rhizome decays, they become separated from the parent plant.

Another mechanism to produce new individual plants takes careful observation to recognize. This is apogamy ("without gametes"). It involves the alternation of sporophytes and gametophytes, but not sexual reproduction. It is interesting because it speaks to the plasticity of plant tissue development. There are several ferns in the following species treatment that are noted as "apogamous," and as having only 32 spores per sporangium, rather than the usual 64 spores found in the higher ferns. (Lower ferns and fern allies have more spores per sporangium.) The spores are produced in the sporangium by five mitotic divisions from the archesporia cell into 2, then 4, then 8, then 16, then 32 cells. These final cells become spores, but without the meiotic reduction division, and therefore, no change in chromosome number. When these spores germinate and grow into tiny gametophyte plants, they may produce sex organs, which are mostly non functional, or they may produce no sex organs at all. Some of these gametophytes reach a stage in metabolic developmental complexity that they act as though they are an embryo, and further development of these gametophytes switches over to sporophyte plant characteristics, eventually maturing to produce spore bearing leaves. Examples of these apogamous ferns are the Black-stemmed Spleenwort (*Asplenium resiliens*), the Purple Cliff-brake (*Pellaea atropurpurea*), and the Woolly Lip Fern (*Cheilanthes tomentosa*). Many ferns adapted to dry habitats are apogamous. They bypass the need for free water for the swimming sperm. Others may have a mixed genetic heritage in their past which makes pairing of their chromosomes difficult or impossible.

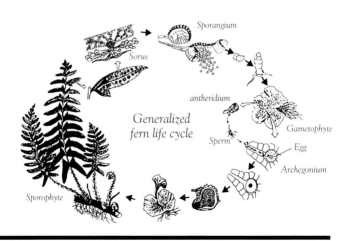

Sporangium

Sorus

antheridium

Gametophyte

Sperm

Egg

Archegonium

Generalized fern life cycle

Sporophyte

Mitotic cell divisions do not necessitate chromosome pairing, whereas meiotic (reduction) division does.

WHAT ARE THE "FERN ALLIES"? . . . .

The fern allies include the club-mosses (*Lycopodium*, in a broad sense), spike-mosses (*Selaginella*), horsetails and scouring rushes (*Equisetum*), quillworts (*Isoetes*), and a few others which are not part of our local flora. Modern studies in plant relationships and diversity show the club-mosses are not as closely related to one another as the common name would imply. The reader will discover in the species treatment that the club-mosses can be divided into several different genera (*Lycopodium*, *Huperzia*, *Diphasiastrum*) even in the Smoky Mountain flora.

The fern allies have a long and rich evolutionary history, and were major elements of what we can loosely refer to as the coal forests of the Carboniferous age of 300-350 million years ago. They are actually older than, and only very distantly related to, ferns. However, there are only about 1,200 species, world wide, in this group, and they are so unrelated to one another and to other major plant groups that they would fall between the cracks, so to speak, if they were not tied with some other larger plant group.

They do have basically the same life cycle as ferns. They are spore bearing plants and have an independent alternation of spore bearing and gamete bearing generations (see The Pteridophyte Life Cycle section above). They are vascular plants as are flowering plants and ferns. They occupy similar positions in the landscape with ferns and they operate ecologically in many similar ways as the ferns.

SEASONS TO ENJOY FERNS . . . .

If you are a student or enthusiast of these plants, then any season is a good season. They are always with us. Some are evergreen, others are deciduous and the leaves die down, turn brown, and wither. But even then many species can be recognized by characteristics of their rhizomes, or their leaves can be recognized by their remains. Forensic botany, so to speak.

That said, the best seasons for learning ferns are late spring through late fall. Our Pteridophytes (literally "fern-plants") are all herbaceous perennials, meaning that their rhizomatous stems live for many years, but their leaves only live for a year or less. The leaves of most go through an elaborate and beautiful unfurling of the croziers, or fiddleheads, as they grow in the spring. This unfurling starts at the base of the leaf blade and progresses outward and upward and takes some time. Also the characteristic sporangia clusters (sori), which are important identification characters, take some time to develop.

For many species of ferns the first leaves to appear do not produce spores, and can be referred to as vegetative leaves, or trophophylls. Fertile leaves, or sporophylls, will be produced later in the growing season. It is as though the plant produces vegetative leaves first, which then provide the plant with sufficient nutrients to produce the reproductive structures (the sporangia full of spores) afterwards. All this takes time, and many ferns are not fully developed until summer.

If you are just getting started learning ferns, it is counter productive to try to learn to recognize plants that are not developed enough to have mature fertile leaves. The same can be said for young plants. The younger the plant the less characteristic the leaf will be, or the less mature the identifying scales or hairs will be. Again, wait until the plant is mature (old) enough to have fertile leaves, then using a hand lens of about 10X you can see important characters and have a good chance of identifying the plant. When you are good at recognizing mature individuals of different species you can play the game of identifying immature individuals.

The same problem arises in reverse in the fall and winter. Evergreen species get more and more worn as winter weathers the plants. The deciduous ferns are going to get beaten down as the weather becomes more unfavorable. Work with what is there as best you can or turn to the evergreen species. Late fall and winter can be good fern hunting seasons because there aren't as many other plants around to distract you. Happy ferning!

PLACES TO LOOK FOR FERNS . . . .

Species abundance of ferns and fern allies is nowhere very high in the Smokies. On a half day hunting expedition, 20 species more or less would be a good day. One needs to try different sorts of ecological habitats, most of them fairly obvious. High elevations, 4,500 feet and above, are places to find boreal species like mountain wood fern, northern beech fern, or running club-moss. Cliffs and ledges are places to find rock ferns like the rock polypody, the spleenworts, cliff-brake, and the lip ferns. High elevation and low elevation rock outcrops are likely to display different species groups. Old fields, former pastures, or overgrown apple orchards are likely places for ferns, particularly some of the small, elusive grapeferns. Swamp forests, particularly at low elevations, display more Southern ferns as well as wide-spread swamp ferns such as the *Osmunda* ferns (cinnamon, interrupted and royal ferns), marsh fern, chain ferns, and log fern. Old home sites can be good hunting if long-ago home owners collected and grew local plants which may persist, if well-adapted to the site.

The Smokies are a wonderful region to study and explore plant and animal diversity. The high elevation mountain tops can be considered biological islands where new species may evolve in isolation from their close relatives. Other species may persist as the climate changes, as has happened since the glacial period. The Smokies were unglaciated but they were much colder than they are today. But even then, regions north of the Smokies were covered with ice and not much of anything grew, so the southern Appalachians became a refugium in which many of the plants one would find further north today survived to repopulate northeastern North America. As long as the weather remains cold enough, many of these "boreal" species still can be found deep in this southern part of North America.

Just a reminder—the Smokies and some nearby mountain ranges have the highest mountains in eastern North America, higher than Mt. Katahdin in Maine or Mt. Washington in New Hampshire, and elevation counts in ecological diversity. As an example, there are many species of *Dryopteris* (the wood ferns) in eastern North America and in the Smokies. One of them, the mountain wood fern (*Dryopteris campyloptera*) occurs above about 5,000 feet in the mountains of Virginia, Tennessee, and North Carolina and then jumps to northern New England and the upper Midwest, where it grows at much lower elevations. The broad beech fern (*Phegopteris hexagonoptera*) is common throughout the rich woods of the southern Appalachians. The northern beech fern (*Phegopteris connectilis*) is widespread in northeastern and central U. S. but its southernmost localities are near a cold waterfall in a gorge near Highlands, North Carolina, and in two places high on Clingmans Dome, in the Smokies.

Some ferns are adapted to the high pH of limestone. There is not very much exposed limestone in the Smokies, but some of the metasedimentary outcrops have a higher pH than others, which may account for occurrences of the walking fern. Mortar in masonry bridges and walls can make good hunting, which can turn up cliffbrakes and unusual fragile ferns. Dry walls, like natural rock outcrops, are fun to explore, but without mortar the natural pH of the stone is not supplemented.

Walking the trails with your eyes glued on the trail sides is rewarding. Mix high elevation and low elevation; sunny dry exposures with Virginia pine vs. rich forests with rhododendron or wildflower glades.

Some trails worth exploring:

◆ The Little River Trail from Elkmont to the Cucumber Gap Trail, or beyond

◆ Around the old homesites in Elkmont (beware of snakes)

◆ Miry Ridge Trail

◆ The Appalachian Trail from Clingmans Dome to Silers Bald

◆ The Appalachian Trail from Newfound Gap to Collins Gap

◆ Baxter Creek Trail from the Big Creek picnic area at least to the sharp west turn above Baxter Creek at about 2,500 feet in elevation

◆ The wet forest (former log ponds) around Big Creek Picnic Area

◆ Marshes, ditches and swamp areas near the gauging station at the Cataloochee Road bridge over Cataloochee Creek, near its junction with Little Cataloochee Creek

◆ The path into low wet woods from the back of the parking lot at The Sinks, on Little River Road

◆ Chestnut Top Trail, from the Townsend "Y" to the top of the ridge

◆ Snake Den Ridge Trail

◆ Brushy Mountain Trail from Trillium Gap to the top of Brushy Mountain, for several club moss species.

Most of these suggested spots have a couple of choice finds, in addition to just being good fern hunting grounds.

All these trails are good spring wildflower trails, but spring wildflower time is not good fern finding time. The possible exception would be to attend the Spring Wildflower Pilgrimage which is put on each year in the Smokies, out of Gatlinburg, which has several fern walks led by competent botanists who can help get you started.

HOW TO USE THIS BOOK . . . .

This book uses lay and general botanical terms for some characteristics (i.e. midrib, petiole, rhizome), and terms more specific to these plants (i.e. rachis, costa, pinna, pinnatifid, strobilus etc.). There is a glossary to guide the reader, with the hope that these terms will insinuate themselves into the reader's consciousness. There are photos taken to emphasize important macroscopic characters. There is a description of each species, including useful identifying characteristics, habitats, and other field notes.

The latinized scientific name is included with each species along with one or more accepted common names. Common names are notoriously variable from region to region and even from one enthusiast to another. The scientific names also change, but follow established international conventions so the names can be traced and verified. Properly, the scientific name is followed by one or more person's names, giving credit to the author(s) of the name, and also aiding in cross checking names. These and other fine points of nomenclature can be found in other floristic manuals, but are omitted here.

A 10X hand lens, and a little practice with it, is a must to see details needed to discriminate species. A more complete regional field guide would be very useful for the serious student. See the included annotated Bibliography.

The Pteridophytes treated in this field guide are arranged in an accepted conventional format. The fern allies are presented first, followed by the more primitive ferns progressing to the more advanced ferns.

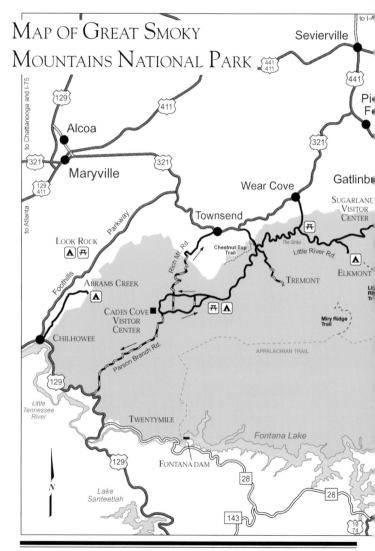

MAP OF GREAT SMOKY
MOUNTAINS NATIONAL PARK

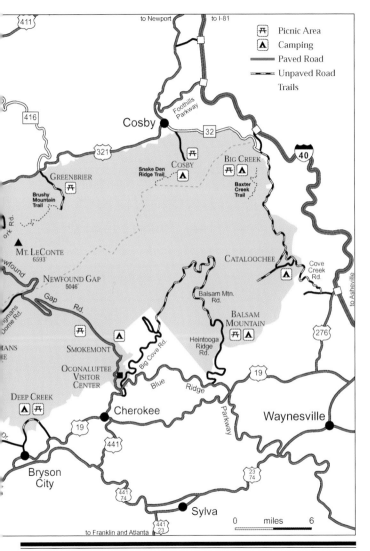

to Newport · to I-81

Picnic Area
Camping
Paved Road
Unpaved Road
Trails

411

416

Cosby   Foothills Parkway

32

40

321

GREENBRIER

Brushy Mountain Trail

Snake Den Ridge Trail

COSBY

BIG CREEK

Baxter Creek Trail

MT. LECONTE
6593'

ork Rd.

wfound

NEWFOUND GAP
5046'

Gap

CATALOOCHEE

Cove Creek Rd.

to Asheville

Balsam Mtn. Rd.

BALSAM MOUNTAIN

Heintooga Ridge Rd.

ighams Dome Rd.

276

HANS E

SMOKEMONT

Big Cove Rd.

OCONALUFTEE VISITOR CENTER

Blue   Ridge

19

DEEP CREEK

or

Cherokee

Parkway

Waynesville

19

441

23 74

Bryson City

441 74

Sylva

to Franklin and Atlanta   441 23

0   miles   6

Ferns & Fern Allies of the Smokies

Huperzia lucidula

Club-moss Family
(*Lycopodiaceae*)

Plant: 5"-8" tall
(12-20 cm)
Leaves: ¼"-⅜" long
(6-10 mm)

Bill Beatty

Individual plants grow in circular clumps, which spread ascending branches that sag down and root to the ground. They do not have distinctive creeping rhizomes, but they often mass into an almost continuous ground cover. The leaves are lance-shaped and produced in tight bushy spirals around the stems. In mature plants, most of the leafy branches bear bands of fertile leaves with single sporangia at the leaf bases; one band per year of growth. The leaves are more shiny than the fir or rock club-mosses, and have small teeth and become wider toward the tip of the leaf.

Although hard to see and requiring magnification, the leaves have stomates only on the underside. Gemmae, or distinctive vegetative buds produced on short branches, are usually produced in only one ring at the top of each stem's annual growth increment.

◆ **STATUS & HABITAT**—This is the most common club-moss in the Smokies, growing from low to mid elevations, in varied cove forests, but particularly as a ground cover in hemlock woods.

APPALACHIAN FIR CLUB-MOSS

Murray Evans

Huperzia appalachiana

Club-moss Family
(*Lycopodiaceae*)

Plant: 2″-4″ tall
(5-10 cm)
Leaves: ⅛″-⅜″ long
(3-10 mm)

This species is similar to, but smaller than, the shining club-moss and grows in a different habitat. Plants grow as small clumps which spread in a circle by ascending branches that do not sag down and root to the ground. They do not have distinctive creeping rhizomes. The leaves are lance-shaped and produced in tight bushy spirals around the stems. In mature plants, most of the leafy branches bear bands of fertile leaves with single sporangia at the leaf bases; one band per year of growth. The leaves are awl-shaped and without teeth. Compared with the shining club-moss, leaves have stomates on both upper and lower surfaces, and have more than 35 stomates on either half of the upper surface.

◆ **STATUS & HABITAT**—This is an uncommon club-moss in the Smokies. It grows as small tufted plants in rock crevices above 6,000 feet in elevation, on headwater streams on peaks such as Mt. Le Conte and Clingmans Dome, and on widely scattered Appalachian peaks in Georgia, North Carolina, Tennessee, and Virginia. They are part of a sensitive alpine flora and need to be left undisturbed. In the southern Appalachians, the Appalachian fir club-moss is disjunct from the principal range of the species from northern New England to Greenland.

Huperzia porophila

Club-moss Family
(*Lycopodiaceae*)

Plant: 4"-6" tall
(10-15 cm)
Leaves: ¼"-⅜" long
(6-10 mm)

Murray Evans

This species is very similar to the Appalachian fir club-moss except for its habitat, its leaves (which have a few low teeth), and the differing stomatal count. Its leaves are awl-shaped, without teeth, or with few irregular low teeth; stomates are on both the upper and lower leaf surfaces, with less than 25 on either half of the upper surface. One to three rings of special vegetative buds (gemmae) are produced near the top of a stem annual growth increment.

◆ **STATUS & HABITAT**—A very rare species that grows on moist, shaded, shale ledges at mid elevations. It is known from a few locations within the Smokies and in nearby North Carolina. It is more common on moist, shaded sandstone ledges on the Cumberland Plateau, in the interior Southeast, and the Midwest.

Running Club-moss

Murray Evans

Lycopodium clavatum

Club-moss Family
(*Lycopodiaceae*)

Plant: 4″-8″ tall
(10-20 cm)
Leaves: ⅛″-¼″ long
(3-6 mm)

This is similar to *Huperzia* in that the plants grow as low evergreen ground cover, and the leaves are bristly and borne in a tight spiral so that the leafy stems appear bushy. However, they differ in several ways. They produce no gemmae. The upright stems fork several times.

The creeping stem (rhizome) is elongated, above ground, with leaves like those of the upright stems. The sporangia are borne singly at the base of the upper surface of specialized leaves. Compared to vegetative leaves without sporangia, the fertile leaves are scale-like and wider and paler, and become yellowish as the sporangia mature. They are aggregated into distinctive cone-like clusters (strobili) ½″-3″ long at the ends of erect leafy stems, which resemble candelabra.

The spores are shed in late fall to early winter. It is distinctive among club-mosses in the forking long-creeping rhizomes which merge with the upright forking stems, both covered with bristly leaves with long hair-like tips.

◆ **STATUS & HABITAT**—An occasional species, it grows in open woods, rocky slopes, balds and along trails at high elevations, but sometimes down to 2,500′.

FLAT-BRANCH GROUND-PINE

Lycopodium obscurum

Club-moss Family
(*Lycopodiaceae*)

Plant: 4"-9" tall
(10-23 cm)
Leaves: ³⁄₁₆" long
(5 mm)

Murray Evans (2)

This plant's upright stems resemble miniature spruce trees. The central erect stem may branch a few times, producing numerous side branches which fork fan-like, parallel to the ground or ascending. Creeping rhizomes are deep underground, with widely spaced thin yellowish leaves.

The leaves of the upright stems are green and needle-like with smooth margins. Leaves of the spreading side branches are arranged in 6 rows around the branch, 2 rows on each side which diverge from the branch, 1 row on top which is somewhat flattened against the branch, and 1 row beneath the branch in which each leaf is only about half as long as those of the other 5 rows, and is flattened against the branch. All are sharp-pointed but without a hair-like tip. Cones are 1"-2½" long arising from tips of erect branches, one to many on each upright stem system. The spores are shed in fall to early winter.

◆ **STATUS & HABITAT**—A frequent species, it grows in open woods, clearings, or balds at mid to high elevations. It's often seen along shrubby rocky trailsides and often with other species of club-mosses.

ROUND-BRANCH GROUND-PINE

Murray Evans

Lycopodium hickeyi

Club-moss Family
(*Lycopodiaceae*)

Plant: 4"-9" tall
(10-23 cm)
Leaves: ³⁄₁₆" long
(5 mm)

This club-moss is much less common than the flat-branch ground-pine. It is the same size, and looks essentially the same in all respects except the leaf orientation on the side branches. The leaves of all 6 rows are the same length, and the upper and lower rows may be flattened against the branch somewhat, but not as much as the flat-branch ground-pine.

The best diagnostic characteristic is the length of the leaves beneath the branch, which are as long as the other rows. But also note that plants of both species growing in sunny, dryer sites will be more erect, more compact, and the leafy branches may be very compact. Consequently, the 6-row orientation and the length of the lower leaves may be hard to determine. Sun-grown plants of both species may superficially resemble this one, and close inspection is necessary.

◆ **STATUS & HABITAT**—This is rare in the Smokies. It occurs on heath balds above 4,000 feet. In some local field manuals this will be listed as *Lycopodium obscurum* var. *isophyllum*.

Lycopodium annotinum

Club-moss Family
(*Lycopodiaceae*)

Plant: 6"-10" tall
(15-25 cm)
Leaves: ³⁄₁₆" long
(5 mm)

Gerald Tang (2)

This club-moss is similar to the flat-branch ground-pine (*Lycopodium obscurum*) but its upright stems are a little taller, stiffly erect, and unbranched. Bristly club-moss leaves are broader than those of flat-branch ground-pine, and bristly club-moss has single cones arising directly from the leafy stem apex.

◆ **STATUS & HABITAT**—This species was collected in 1899 by Albert Ruth from the summit of Thunderhead Mountain on the Tennessee-North Carolina state line and has not been seen since. It is presumed to no longer occur in the Smokies. It occurs in Virginia and West Virginia, so it could be rediscovered in the park.

SOUTHERN RUNNING-CEDAR

David Duhl

Diphasiastrum digitatum

Club-moss Family
(*Lycopodiaceae*)

Plant: 6"-10" tall
Leaves: ¹⁄₁₆"-¹⁄₈" long
(1.5-3 mm)

Southern running-cedar is composed of horizontal spreading stems (rhizomes) creeping on the surface or in the leaf litter. The widely-spaced vertical stem complexes fork several times, ultimately producing fan-like lateral branches, either ascending or horizontal to the ground. The foliage is a rich green. The lateral branches may grow for several years and the small joint that forms at the end of each growing season is inconspicuous and not pinched.

The leaves of the terminal branchlets are 4-ranked and scale-like, the 2 on the sides larger than the rows on the upperside and underside of the branch. The leaf bases are overlapping and shingle-like. The overlapping shingle-like scale leaves are the most diagnostic character to differentiate *Diphasiastrum* from *Lycopodium*. Its cones are usually 2 or 4, resembling a candelabra, on distinctive stalks arising from upper leafy branches.

♦ **STATUS & HABITAT**—Common from low to high elevations, often in dry, rocky woods and around old homesites. This species and *Lycopodium obscurum* are often collected for Christmas greens, much to the detriment of these very slow-growing plants.

Diphasiastrum
tristachyum

Club-moss Family
(*Lycopodiaceae*)

Plant: 6"-10" tall
Leaves: 1/16"-1/8" long
(1.5-3 mm)

Murray Evans

This species has the same size and appearance and is very similar to Southern running-cedar except: the foliage is blue-green rather than true green, the rhizomes are generally deep underground, and the annual growth increments on the leafy side branches are conspicuously pinched. Also, the side branches tend to grow in an ascending cone-like pattern, rather than the more flat, fan-like pattern of Southern running-cedar. It is the same size as the preceding, or somewhat more compact and smaller.

The common names of all the club-mosses are confusingly interwoven. Pick the one you like from a manual you have confidence in. The new divisions of the broad classic *Lycopodium* have a logic and a system that makes sense.

◆ **STATUS & HABITAT**—This species is less common than Southern running-cedar, grows in smaller clumps, and tends to grow on dryer, more exposed sites. Look for it on heath balds, rock ledges, and exposed southerly trail sides at mid elevations.

MEADOW SPIKE-MOSS

Murray Evans

Selaginella apoda

Spike-moss Family
(*Selaginellaceae*)

Plant: 1″ tall
(2.5 cm)
Leaves: ¹⁄₁₆″ long
(1.5 mm)

Meadow spike-mosses are inconspicuous matted plants which lie on, or close to, the ground around other vegetation. They superficially resemble mosses, but have true stems, which mosses lack. The stems are horizontal, delicate, ¹⁄₁₆″ in diameter, and fork repeatedly. They bear 4 rows of delicate pale green scale-like leaves in an unusual arrangement. There are two lateral rows of ovate leaves ¹⁄₁₆″ long and less wide, 1 on each side, which diverge at a wide angle from the stem. Two rows of smaller narrower leaves on top of the stems lie more or less parallel to the stem on top of the lateral rows.

The strobili (cones) are similar to those of the club-mosses, with several significant differences. Some leafy branch tips become fertile, and the scale leaves produce single sporangia at their bases. The strobilus has two kinds of sporangia. A few at the base of the strobilus have 4 or fewer relatively large megaspores. The rest of the sporangia are smaller, but contain hundreds of microspores.

♦ **STATUS & HABITAT**—Probably less scarce than generally considered due to its inconspicuous habit. Grows in wet meadows and margins of ponds and marshy streams at low elevations.

Selaginella rupestris

Spike-moss Family (*Selaginellaceae*)

Plant: 1"-2" tall
Leaves: ¹⁄₁₆" long
(1.5 mm)

Murray Evans

Although this species has not been documented in the Smokies, it occurs in the mountains around the park, particularly in North Carolina. It has quite a different aspect than meadow spike-moss. The leaves are spirally arranged, dark green, and stiff with a straight bristle tip. The branches are tufted and ascending, making the plants resemble tiny club-mosses. The fertile leaves are 4-ranked producing a 4-angled strobilus at the tips of some branches. There are a few large-spored megasporangia at the base of the strobilus and lots of small-spored microsporangia above.

◆ **STATUS & HABITAT**—Not yet documented in the Great Smoky Mountains. Rock spike-moss carpets exposed ledges at mid to high elevations.

An additional species endemic to the mountains of western North Carolina, northwest South Carolina and north Georgia, but not yet known from the Smokies, is the twisted-hair spike-moss (*Selaginella tortipila*). It is the same size and appearance as rock spike-moss, and occupies the same habitat; it differs in that the leaf bristle tip is longer and twisted.

CAROLINA QUILLWORT

Isoetes valida

Quillwort Family
(Isoetaceae)

Leaves: up to
20″ long
(51 cm)

Murray Evans (2)

This plant is aquatic, submerged or emergent, tufted, and rush-like. The stem is a short, erect, fleshy underground globose tuber ⅓″-½″ in diameter with roots arising from the base and sides and leaves arising from the flattened top. The leaves are erect and firm or limp when submerged; linear, bright green, round in cross-section, with lengthwise strengthening partitions, and a single vascular bundle up the middle of the leaf. The leaf base is pale, flattened, and dilated.

In fertile leaves, the base contains a large sporangium imbedded in a cavity in the submerged and underground leaf base. The velum (an eyelid-like partial covering over the cavity in the leaf base in which the sporangium is borne) covers about 75% of the sporangium. Megasporangia contain hundreds of large white megaspores.

◆ **STATUS & HABITAT**—In the Smokies, it is commonly found in ditches and boggy areas along Cataloochee Creek, Cataloochee group camp, and ditches along Raven Fork. Grows emergent in ponds, slow moving streams, ditches, bogs, and seeps from low to high elevations. The plant size depends on habitat. Several recent manuals refer to this species as *Isoetes caroliniana*.

*Isoetes
appalachiana*

Quillwort Family
(*Isoetaceae*)

Leaves: 8"-20" long
(20-51 cm)

W. Carl Taylor

Appalachian quillwort is similar to Carolina quillwort in most respects. However, the Appalachian quillwort has the following characteristics that differentiate it: the underground tuberous stem is ½"-1" in diameter, the leaves are erect or spreading, the sporangium wall is streaked with brown pigment, and the megaspore wall ornamentation is a more irregular network (cristate-reticulate) of ragged-edged plates of variable height. Also, in the Appalachian quillwort, the partial covering over the sporangia (velum) covers only about 25% of the sporangium, whereas it covers about 75% of the sporangium in the Carolina quillwort.

◆ **STATUS & HABITAT**—In the Smokies, this species is currently known as a submerged or emergent species in or around ponds and streams in Cades Cove.

The Appalachian and Carolina quillwort are two of several species in the eastern U. S. which have been separated out of a broadly inclusive aggregate species *Isoetes engelmannii* (Engelmann's quillwort), which is found in the Smokies near Fontana Lake.

FIELD HORSETAIL

Equisetum arvense

Horsetail Family
(*Equisetaceae*)

Plants: up to 2′ tall
(61 cm)

These plants are distinctive in their unusual jointed green stems with small scale-like leaves in a crown encircling each stem joint. The black wiry rhizomes are deep underground. The stems are ribbed vertically and contain silica in the tissues so they feel coarse and scratchy; hence "scouring" from early use as pot scrubbers. The stems are deciduous, about ⅛″ in diameter, with rings of lateral branches arising from all but a few basal and apical stem joints; the lateral branches themselves are unbranched, but ridged and jointed similar to the main stem. The fertile stems appear in the early spring, are 4″ to 8″ tall, ephemeral, pinkish, and unbranched, with a terminal cone of many shield-like scale leaves. The sporangia are borne on the underside of these distinctive umbrella-like scale leaves of the cone (strobilus). The fertile stems die down after the spores are shed.

The evergreen unbranched scouring rush, *Equisetum hyemale*, occurs sporadically around the park on river and lakeshores, ditches, marshes, roadsides, and waste places.

♦ **STATUS & HABITAT**—Field horsetail occurs sporadically on roadsides, stream banks, wet meadows, and old fields at low elevations.

Botrychium virginianum

Grapefern Family
(*Ophioglossaceae*)

Plant: 3″-1½′ tall
(8-46 cm)

Rebecca Schillett

Fertile rattlesnake ferns have an enormous range in size. Plants of varying sizes often grow together in large populations. The small fleshy stems (rhizomes) are underground and appear mostly as pale spreading cord-like roots. The rhizomes do not spread, so the plant grows in place and produces usually only a single leaf each year. The vegetative blade of the leaf is light green, herbaceous, broadly triangular in outline, and about 3 times dissected. The ultimate segments have a ragged-toothed outline. The leaf blade is usually angled more or less horizontally to the ground from the top of the common petiole.

There is usually a single fertile complex, which is erect and about as long as the vegetative leaf blade, and has a regular series of lateral branches. The branches are covered with large short-stalked sporangia lined up along the side branches. The plants appear above ground in early spring and shed their spores in late spring, at which time the fertile complex withers, leaving the vegetative portion of the leaf until it withers in fall.

♦ **STATUS & HABITAT**—Common in rich woods at low to mid elevations. This is the largest and most common of the grapeferns.

COMMON GRAPE FERN

Botrychium dissectum

Grapefern Family
(*Ophioglossaceae*)

Leaves: 6"-10" tall
(15-25 cm)

Murray Evans (2)

The rhizome is underground, fleshy, and does not spread, appearing mostly as many spreading cord-like roots. It produces one leaf per year. Many leaves are not fertile and produce no sporangia, but for those that are fertile, the common petiole divides close to the ground, giving rise to two distinctively different parts of one leaf. One is a long-stalked erect fertile complex of many ascending branches covered with globose sporangia resembling a massive upright bunch of grapes.

The other is a long-stalked triangular dissected vegetative blade. The vegetative leaf blade is dark green, often becoming bronze in winter or when in bright sun. The vegetative blade can be of two forms, even in the same population. One form is highly dissected so as to be skeletonized, but still of a green leaf texture. The common form is triangular in outline with two large basal pinnae, each nearly the size and complexity of the rest of the leaf blade.

Common grape ferns remain green over the winter.

◆ **STATUS & HABITAT**—They are common, and occur in low to mid elevation, in old fields, old orchards, disturbed woods or alluvial woods. They often grow in company with other species of *Botrychium*.

*Botrychium
biternatum*

Grapefern Family
(*Ophioglossaceae*)

Leaves: 6″-10″ tall
(15-25 cm)

Murray Evans

Southern grape fern is very similar in appearance and size to the common grape fern except: it does not display the dissected skeletonized vegetative blade form; it is only 2 times, or rarely 3 times, dissected; and the innermost downward pointing pinnules of the basal pinnae have only 1 elongate segment with a more rounded apex. The whole vegetative leaf blade has fewer leaf segments and has a more open appearance.

Southern and common grape ferns are not easy to differentiate except for the more extreme forms; most dissected or most lobed with more angular leaf segments in the common grape fern and least lobed with more rounded leaf segments and more open in appearance in the southern grape fern.

Like the common grape fern, it appears in summer, sheds spores in fall, remains green through winter, and dies down in spring.

♦ **STATUS & HABITAT**—Southern grape fern may grow alone in pure stands, or it may grow mixed with the common grape fern. It is less common than the common grape fern, but grows in similar habitats.

DAISY-LEAVED MOONWORT

Murray Evans

*Botrychium
matricariifolium*

Grapefern Family
(*Ophioglossaceae*)

Leaves: 2″-8″ tall
(5-20 cm)

The leaves are light green, small, narrow, and inconspicuous. They grow, only one per year, from unbranched underground rhizomes with cord-like roots. The common petiole is tall and only ¹⁄₁₆″ in diameter. The light green vegetative blade diverges close under the erect fertile complex, which has several pairs of forking lateral stalks each with a few large spherical sporangia. The vegetative blade is half as long as the fertile complex, short stalked, oblong (ovate) in outline, once pinnate, with several pairs of lateral leaflets (pinnae), that are irregularly toothed or lobed.

This moonwort is inconspicuous and doesn't really look like a fern with its thin round stalk, a little tuft of green leafy material on one side, and a little cluster of grape-like sporangia at the apex of the plant. The leaves die down in late summer.

◆ **STATUS & HABITAT**—Rare in our area, it grows in old fields or disturbed woods at low elevation. Here is the southern limit of its range. This species usually grows in large populations of many individuals, even though the rhizomes do not spread and produce more plants vegetatively. It often grows with other *Botrychiums*.

LANCE-LEAVED MOONWORT

Botrychium
lanceolatum subsp.
angustisegmentum

Grapefern Family
(*Ophioglossaceae*)

Leaves: 3"-10" tall
(8-25 cm)

Murray Evans

The leaves of this fern are dark green, smaller, narrower, and more inconspicuous than the very similar daisy-leaved moonwort. The leaves grow singly from the underground, unbranched rhizome, and are narrow and wiry so as to be difficult to find. The spore bearing leaf part (fertile complex) is unbranched, or few branched, with two sparse rows of spherical sporangia 1/32" in diameter on each branch and partially immersed in the branches. The vegetative blade arises directly below the fertile complex, at right angles to the petiole, and is triangular in outline with a few narrow linear lobes less than 1/8" wide with irregularly cut or sharply toothed margins.

◆ **STATUS & HABITAT**—Rare in our area, it grows in disturbed woods at low elevation. It is even less common and grows in smaller populations than daisy-leaved moonwort. The leaves appear in late spring; spores are shed in summer, and the leaves die down in early fall. The Smokies are nearly the southern limit of its range.

SOUTHERN ADDER'S-TONGUE

Murray Evans

Ophioglossum vulgatum

Grapefern Family
(Ophioglossaceae)

Leaves: 6"-8" tall
(15-20 cm)

These ferns are related to the grape ferns, with some similarities and some striking visual differences. They have small soft fleshy underground rhizomes with cord-like roots, and they sometimes spread and produce new plants from vegetative buds underground. The leaves grow singly from each rhizome each year, and are of two quite different parts, as in the grape ferns. The vegetative portion is an undivided smooth, shiny spoon-like elliptical blade 1" to 1½" wide by 3"-4" long, with a smooth margin and no hairs or scales. The veins of the leaf blade are a network of polygons. The spore bearing leaf part (the fertile complex) is on a long erect stalk rising above the base of the blade, the top of which is somewhat flattened, and has large sporangia fused together in two partially buried rows.

◆ **STATUS & HABITAT**—These plants are not particularly uncommon, but are difficult to spot. They may grow in populations of dozens or even hundreds, but the stalked fertile complexes are delicate and inconspicuous, and the leaf blades look like lots of other ground cover plants. They grow in disturbed woods, along wooded streams, old fields and roadsides, at low to mid elevations.

CINNAMON FERN

Osmunda cinnamomea

Royal Fern Family
(*Osmundaceae*)

Leaves: 2'-4' tall
(0.6-1.2 meters)

Rebecca Schillett

This big fern displays tall leaves arranged in a circle like a crown. They are light green, deciduous, 6"-12" wide, once divided, and the leaflets are deeply lobed (pinnate-pinnatifid). Each lobe is rounded but slightly pointed at the end. Each lateral pinna has an inconspicuous fuzzy collar around the midrib where it joins the leaf rachis. They are without scales, but have matted cinnamon colored hairs, particularly on young leaves.

The rhizomes are woody and partially exposed above ground, but imbedded in a dense mass of black, wiry roots. Sporangia are borne on skeletonized, completely fertile leaves standing tall in the center of the circle of green vegetative leaves, without green leaf blade tissue. The sporangia are intermediate in size and structure between the grape ferns and most other ferns. The fertile leaves turn cinnamon brown and wither in late spring when the spores are shed. The spores are green, which is unusual in ferns, occurring only in *Osmunda* and *Onoclea*, the sensitive fern.

◆ **STATUS & HABITAT**—Common in swamps, marshes, bottomland woods, stream sides, and seeps at low to high elevation.

INTERRUPTED FERN

Osmunda claytoniana

Royal Fern Family
(*Osmundaceae*)

Leaves: 2'-4' tall
(0.6-1.2 meters)

Murray Evans (2)

The interrupted fern is like the cinnamon fern in size, shape, and habit, except the lobes of the vegetative leaflets (pinnae) are rounded and not slightly pointed, and the collar at the base of the pinna is not fuzzy. Most conspicuously, the skeletonized fertile pinnae are not on separate leaves but are several adjacent pinna pairs in the middle of otherwise typical vegetative leaves. When the spores are shed the pinnae are also shed, leaving an "interrupted" space in the leaf.

◆ **STATUS & HABITAT**—Interrupted fern is a northern species that is much less common here than the cinnamon fern. It also prefers swamps, marshes, wet woods, and seeps from low to high elevations. Whereas the cinnamon fern and the royal fern occur all along eastern and central North America from Florida and Texas to Ontario and Newfoundland, the southern limits of this species are just south of the Smokies.

ROYAL FERN

Osmunda regalis

Royal Fern Family
(*Osmundaceae*)

Leaves: 2'-5' tall
(0.6-1.5 meters)

judywhite/GardenPhotos

Rebecca Schillett

Royal fern is related to the preceding cinnamon and interrupted ferns. Its growth habit, size, and its rhizome characteristics are similar to the cinnamon and interrupted ferns, but the leaves appear quite different and grow in less symmetrical crowns. The leaf blade is two-thirds as wide as it is long, is 2-pinnate, and the leaflets are oblong, stalked, and widely separated along the pinna midrib. The individual leaflets correspond to the pinna lobes in the cinnamon and interrupted ferns, and all three species have the same venation pattern. The royal fern does not have the collar of hairs at the pinna base where it joins the leaf midrib. The fertile leaves have vegetative pinnae toward the leaf base and several skeletonized fertile pinnae with sporangia borne along the pinna branches at the leaf apex.

◆ **STATUS & HABITAT**—Infrequent, in swamps, marshes, or stream banks at low to mid elevations. It is most often seen in woods and marshes along streams. The leaves will be shorter and more clumped in locations with more light, and appear larger and more limp when growing in deep shade.

CLIMBING FERN

Lygodium
palmatum

Climbing Fern Family
(*Lygodiaceae*)

Leaves: 6'-8' long
(1.8-2.4 meters)

Rebecca Schiflett (2)

This is a most unusual fern that climbs like Japanese honeysuckle, only not by stems, but by the twining leaf rachis.

The rhizome is wiry, spreads near the surface of the ground in the leaf litter, and is covered with dark brown hairs, but no scales. Its leaves arise 1"-2" apart along the rhizome, spreading on the ground or climbing any available support by their twining midrib. The lower leaflets are vegetative, palmately lobed like a hand with 4-6 extended fingers. These leaflets are in pairs, on short stalks, joined to the leaf midrib by a common stalk. The fertile pinnae are at the apex of the leaf and are highly contracted, but with some green leaf tissue remaining. The sporangia are borne on the underside of the "fingers," in two rows, on each side of the midvein, and each is covered by a delicate flap of tissue like a pocket (the indusium).

◆ **STATUS & HABITAT**—Occurs at low to mid elevations, is widely scattered, and is encountered in small populations unexpectedly along trails, usually in open brushy sites. There is a large population on Little River Road between Sugarlands Visitor Center and Elkmont Campground.

*Adiantum
pedatum*

Maidenhair Fern
Family
(*Adiantaceae*)

Plants: 8″-20″ tall
(20-50 cm)

Murray Evans

This species is easily recognized by its shiny purple leaf axes and the graceful flat footprint-like leaf outline. It has leaves with stiff, polished, blackish petioles up to 14″ long, with a few narrow brown scales toward the base. Its rhizome is short-creeping and branching, ⅛″ in diameter, and covered with brown lanceolate scales. The midrib first divides equally at the apex of the petiole to form the two halves of the leaf. It then unequally divides, forming the fan-shaped leaf outline with many delicate bright green triangular to oblong leaflets on short stiff black stalks. Sporangia are clustered in short patches under the scalloped outer edges of many of the leaflets. They are covered by the folded over edges of the leaflets (false indusium).

◆ **STATUS & HABITAT**—Frequent from low to mid elevations, in rich rocky woods, or on moist ledges.

   The three local genera of the Adiantaceae Family, the maiden-hair ferns (*Adiantum*), the lip ferns (*Cheilanthes*), and the cliff-brakes (*Pellaea*) are quite distinct from each other.

ALABAMA LIP FERN

Murray Evans

Cheilanthes alabamensis

Maidenhair Fern Family
(*Adiantaceae*)

Leaves: 3"-10" tall
(8-25 cm)

Rebecca Schiflett

This is a rock fern of dry calcareous (limestone) places: cliffs, quarries or road cuts. Its rhizomes are clustered, short-creeping, branching, densely brown scaly. Its leaf petioles are about half as long as the leaf blade, lustrous black, wiry, polished, and sparsely hairy. The axes within the blade are like the petiole. The leaf blade is lanceolate, dark green, and very sparsely hairy on upper and lower surfaces. It is 2-pinnate, or 1-pinnate with pinna segments cut to the pinna midrib. The segments are lanceolate and pointed. The sporangia are in elongated, nearly continuous sori under the edge of the leaf segments and more or less covered by the rolled-over edge of the segment margin. There are only 32 spores in each sporangium, indicating that these plants are apogamous (see the Fern Life Cycle section).

◆ **STATUS & HABITAT**—This species grows at low elevation, but is rare, growing on calcareous cliffs and ledges, which are not common in the Smokies. Calcareous outcrops are more common in the Tennessee River valley and the Cumberland Plateau.

There are three species of *Cheilanthes* within the Smokies, all rare and in small populations.

Cheilanthes lanosa

Maidenhair Fern Family
(*Adiantaceae*)

Leaves: 4"-10" tall
(10-25 cm)

Hairy lip fern is similar to the Alabama lip fern in habit, size, and shape. However, the hairy lip fern has leaves that are grey green in color, with the leaf axes dark brown, and the leaves are 4"-10" tall. The petiole is ⅔ as long as the blade. The petioles and blades are not scaly, but have conspicuous twisted hairs; the leaf segments are less hairy on top than beneath. The leaves are 2-pinnate with the ultimate segments oblong with rounded apex ⅛" long and broadly attached to their common stalk. The sori are on the edge of the underside of the leaf with the leaf margin partially rolled over the line of sporangia. The sporangia are shiny black when mature and have 64 spores (see the Alabama and woolly lip ferns and the Fern Life Cycle section).
♦ **STATUS & HABITAT**—Rare in the Smokies. Plants of low elevation on dry, acidic, shale cliffs and ledges.

WOOLLY LIP FERN

Cheilanthes tomentosa

Maidenhair Fern Family
(*Adiantaceae*)

Leaves: 4"-10" tall
(10-25 cm)

Murray Evans

Rebecca Shiflett

The woolly lip fern is similar to the hairy lip fern in habit, size, shape and color. The leaf is 1½" to 2½" wide, with the petiole about two-thirds as long as the blade. The leaf blade is light green and sparsely hairy above and densely woolly below. It is also scaly with light brown scales with a darker brown central stripe. The hairs and scales are whitish when young and become reddish brown when older, making the leaf underside russet colored. The leaf blades are 3-pinnate, the ultimate, or final, segments are less than ⅛" in diameter, round to oblong, and pinched at the base so as to appear bead-like. Sporangia are borne in marginal sori as in the hairy lip fern, with 32 spores (thereby having an apogamous life cycle).

♦ **STATUS & HABITAT**—Plants of low elevation, on dry acidic ledges and cliffs. Rare in the Smokies.

*Pellaea
atropurpurea*

Maidenhair Fern Family
(*Adiantaceae*)

Leaves: 4″-20″ tall
(10-50 cm)

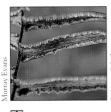

This fern has compact branching rhizomes with reddish brown scales. Its leaves have petioles equaling or shorter than the blade. The petioles are stiff, wiry, glossy purple to blackish, sparsely hairy. The leaf blades are 2″-4″ wide, narrowly triangular, evergreen, stiff, brittle, 2-pinnate at blade base, 1-pinnate toward apex. The segments are wide-spaced, stalked, and dark green. The sporangia are in elongate sori running the length of the segment margins, covered by the rolled over leaf margin. The sporangia have 32 spores. The fertile leaves tend to be taller and more erect with narrower leaf segments than the shorter and spreading purely vegetative leaves.

♦ **STATUS & HABITAT**—Plants of low elevation on dry, limestone cliffs, ledges, and boulders. Also masonry walls. Uncommon in the Smokies. Look in the masonry on the cool shady surfaces of stone bridges.

DWARF BRISTLE FERN

Trichomanes petersii

Filmy Fern Family
(*Hymenophyllaceae*)

Leaf: blades ¼" long
(6 mm)

Murray Evans (2)

Dwarf bristle ferns look more like a large moss or leafy liverwort than a fern, but the thread-like black hairy rhizomes and forking veins in the leaves indicate that it is a fern. The petiole is as long as the leaf blade; the leaves make an overlapping shingle-like mat generally less then ½" high. The blade is elliptical, only one cell thick, and the margin is smooth or undulate with stiff black hairs (seen with a 10X hand lens). The sorus is also unique among ferns. It is at the tip of the midvein of some leaves and consists of a hollow cone partially imbedded in the leaf with a bristle extension of the midvein inside the cone, on which sporangia are borne.

◆ **STATUS & HABITAT**—Rare and easily overlooked, it grows on shaded, moist, granitic boulders and cliff crevices at low elevations. Most filmy ferns require an environment with high humidity.

There are two genera of filmy ferns, *Hymenophyllum* and *Trichomanes*, with several species in the southern Appalachians, and three species in the Smokies. Two species occur only as independent vegetatively reproduced gametophyte colonies (see p. 84).

*Dennstaedtia
punctilobula*

Bracken Fern Family
(*Dennstaedtiaceae*)

Leaves: 1½'-3' tall
(0.45-0.9 meter)

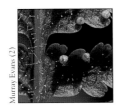

Murray Evans (2)

Hay-scented ferns have leaves that are highly dissected and thin textured, forming dense clumps and sometimes whole fern glades. The
rhizomes are deep underground, red-brown, and hairy. The leaves are
3-pinnate, narrowly triangular, widest at, or near, the base of the
blade. The petiole is red brown at its base and greenish above, and
about half the length of the blade. The sori are small, beside a notch
in the leaf segment margin. The indusium is around the sorus rather
than over it, and is composed of a flap of leaf margin fused with a true
indusium forming a cup, like tiny tea cups. The whole leaf is covered
with silvery, stalked, glandular hairs.

The Bracken Fern Family is characterized as large plants, with
hairs but not scales, and marginal sori.

◆ **STATUS & HABITAT**—The plants are common, in a wide range
of elevations and habitats, including old fields, dry woods, slopes,
roadsides, and stream banks.

BRACKEN FERN

*Pteridium
aquilinum*

Bracken Fern Family
(*Dennstaedtiaceae*)

Leaves: 1½'-4' tall
(0.45-1.2 meters)

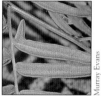

judywhite/GardenPhotos

Murray Evans

Bracken fern leaves are erect, coarse, stiff, and leathery. The coarse, black, hairy rhizome is deep underground and spreads aggressively in suitable habitats. The petiole is as long as the blade, reddish toward the base and green above. The blade is broadly triangular or ovate. The two basal pinnae are almost as large as the rest of the blade and project forward, often turning the blade almost parallel to the ground. The blade is 2-pinnate-pinnatifid to 3-pinnate; the ultimate lobes oblong to linear. The sori are elongate under the segment margins covered by the rolled-over leaf margin.

Two varieties can be recognized in our area, with some difficulty. The more northern eastern bracken (var. *latiusculum*) has the longest ultimate segments 4 times as long as broad, with moderately hairy margins. The more southern tailed bracken (var. *pseudocaudatum*) has ultimate segments 6-15 times as long as broad, with margins glabrous to only slightly hairy.

◆ **STATUS & HABITAT**—Bracken ferns are common in disturbed areas, thickets, roadsides, and persist in dry open woods. As the forests mature, this fern of open habitats becomes less frequent.

Thelypteris novaboracensis

Marsh Fern Family
(*Thelypteridaceae*)

Leaf: blades 6″-20″ long
(15-51 cm)

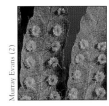

Murray Evans (2)

New York fern is easily recognized by its pale green color, delicate appearance, and especially by the leaf blade that tapers to a point at the tip and nearly so at the base. Its leaves are deciduous and grow in clumps of 4 to 6, spaced ½″-1″ apart. New York ferns are usually found in large populations of many leaf clusters, mostly connected by the underground, blackish, creeping, branching rhizomes with light brown scales near the branch apex. The petiole is less than ¼ the length of the blade, light green or straw colored, with a few delicate ovate light- to reddish-brown scales. The blade is narrowly lanceolate and tapering conspicuously to short pinnae less than ½″ long at the base of the blade. The pinnae with elongate pinna lobes cut nearly to the pinna midrib (pinnate-pinnatifid), and the lateral veinlets of these lobes are unforked. The leaf tissue is silvery hairy. The sori are small, horse-shoe shaped (reniform), with delicate hairy indusia.

◆ **STATUS & HABITAT**—Common in a wide range of habitats: woods, swamps, and moist old fields, at low to mid elevations, often in large populations.

MARSH FERN

Thelypteris palustris

Marsh Fern Family
(*Thelypteridaceae*)

Leaf: blades 6″-20″ long
(15-51 cm)

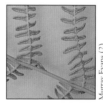

Murray Evans (2)

Marsh fern leaves are clumped as in the New York fern and are about the same height. However, the lowest pinnae are nearly as long as the longest, and the leaves are dimorphic with the fertile leaves taller and narrower than the vegetative leaves. Also, the margins of the fertile pinna lobes are rolled under somewhat, making the fertile leaves appear conspicuously more open. The lateral veinlets of the pinna lobes are forked, and the leaf tissue is less hairy than the New York fern; the sori are similar.

♦ **STATUS & HABITAT**—This is much less common than the New York fern, and found in wetter sites at low elevations such as swamps and marshes. Its leaves may be seen standing upright among grasses and sedges.

The more northern bog fern (*Thelypteris simulata*) is rare in the southern Appalachians south of West Virginia; currently known only from near Pineola in Avery County, North Carolina. There is a 1931 collection reported to be from a creekside near Pigeon Forge, Tennessee.

Phegopteris hexagonoptera

Marsh Fern Family
(*Thelypteridaceae*)

Leaves: 7″-15″ tall
(18-38 cm)

Murray Evans (2)

Broad beech fern leaves are deciduous, growing ½″ or more apart along the branching, creeping, scaly, underground rhizome. The petiole is slender and brittle and 1½ to 2 times as long as the blade. The leaf blade is usually angled nearly parallel to the ground from the apex of the petiole, is 5″-12″ long, triangular, and as wide as, or wider than, long. The pinna lobes are broadly attached to the pinna midrib, and the pinnae attach broadly to the rachis forming an undulating wing along the leaf midrib. The leaf tissue has moderately short transparent hairs, and also short-stalked glandular hairs, and a few whitish lanceolate scales. The sori are small, round, without indusium, and are about halfway between the midvein and the margin of the pinna lobes.

♦ **STATUS & HABITAT**—This species is common throughout the region, occurring at low to mid elevations in rich woods and river bottoms.

Many identification manuals combine *Phegopteris* in *Thelypteris* from which *Phegopteris* can be separated based on lacking the indusium, among other technical characteristics.

NORTHERN BEECH FERN

Phegopteris connectilis

Marsh Fern Family
(*Thelypteridaceae*)

Leaves: 7"-15" tall
(18-38 cm)

Murray Evans (2)

This species differs from the broad beech fern in several ways. The leaf is about the same size, but the blades are less broad and about 1½ times as long as wide. The blade is firmer, more erect, more conspicuously hairy on the leaf tissue, and more scaly on the axes. The lowest pinna pair tends to angle forward; and, particularly, the rachis wing above the lowest pinna pair is discontinuous, so as to separate the lowest pair from the rest of the pinnae of the leaf blade.

The leaves of both this and the southern beech fern tend to be reddish in the spring and turn reddish or pale yellow before they wither in the fall.

♦ **STATUS & HABITAT**—This species is common in the northeastern U. S. and across Canada, but reaches its southern limit here. It is found in high elevation rocky woods and ledges. In the park it occurs only in one remote population on Mt. Le Conte, one remote population on the Tennessee side of Clingmans Dome, and one site on top of a cliff above the Clingmans Dome Road in North Carolina.

In many identification guides this species is listed as *Thelypteris phegopteris*.

*Woodwardia
areolata*

Chain Fern Family
(*Blechnaceae*)

Leaves: 2′-2 ½′ tall
(61-76 cm)

Rebecca Schillett

This fern is deciduous. Its rhizome is coarse, long-creeping, and sparsely scaly with brown scales. The leaves are reddish-bronze in spring, becoming green, broadly lanceolate, pinnatifid—the pinnae joining a broad wing along the rachis; dimorphic, the vegetative leaves shorter, with broader segments and appearing earlier in spring.

The fertile leaves are taller and erect, the segments narrower with wide spaces between segments. Venation of the leaf tissue is conspicuously netted. The sori are large, elongate, in two chains—one on either side of the pinna midrib like links of sausage, the smooth domed indusium attached along the side. With the long sori, there is a distinctive "chain" of elongate cells along the segment midribs from which the common name is derived. The leaves turn yellow in fall.

◆ **STATUS & HABITAT**—Netted chain ferns are widely scattered in localized populations in low elevation swamps and wet woods.

VIRGINIA CHAIN FERN

Murray Evans

Woodwardia virginica

Chain Fern Family
(*Blechnaceae*)

Leaves: 2'-4' tall
(0.6-1.2 meters)

This fern is deciduous, its rhizome stout, up to ⅜″ in diameter, with scales few and dark reddish brown. Its leaves are erect, bronze when young, becoming green and turning yellow in the fall. The petiole is as long as the blade, dark and scaly at the base. The blade is 1'-2' long, the pinna lobes triangular, deeply lobed, and broadly attached (pinnate-pinnatifid) to the pinna midrib (costa), which is sparsely scaly, particularly when young. The veins of the leaf are characteristic, fusing into a single chain on each side of the pinna costae and the segment midveins, from which side veinlets diverge straight to the segment margin. The sori follow the midveins, as in the netted chain fern, but are shorter and smaller.

◆ **STATUS & HABITAT**—This fern grows in marshes or swamp woods. It is rare in this region, and the only known park locality is in a wooded swampy pond in Cades Cove, where it has not been recently seen. It is more common on the southeastern coastal plain. It somewhat resembles the cinnamon fern (*Osmunda cinnamomea*), which has pale petiole bases and mats of long cinnamon-colored hairs and no scales.

Asplenium rhizophyllum

Spleenwort Family
(*Aspleniaceae*)

Leaves: 3"-1' tall
(8-30 cm)

Walking fern leaves are evergreen, spreading or arching from a small erect rhizome; the short petioles are green with a glossy brown base. The leaf blades are undivided, heart-shaped at the base, and either lanceolate with a bluntly pointed apex or up to 1' long, and tapered to a long tail-like apex. The long-tailed leaves frequently root at the tip and produce new plants, thus "walking" over the ground. The leaf veins form a network of irregular large areolae; the sori are elongate and of varying length and follow this irregular network, as does the elongate indusium.

♦ **STATUS & HABITAT**—This striking small fern makes mats of plants both by rhizome branching and by leaf tip "walking." It grows primarily on limestone, but will also grow on calcified rock types that are otherwise acidic, and on tree bases. It is sporadic and unpredictable at low to mid elevations, but not rare in the Smokies.

EBONY SPLEENWORT

Asplenium platyneuron

Spleenwort Family
(*Aspleniaceae*)

Leaves: 3″-1′ tall
(8-30 cm)

Murray Evans (2)

Ebony spleenwort leaves are light green, semi-evergreen, and dimorphic. The vegetative leaves are short, more compact, and arching close to the substrate. The fertile leaves are much taller (up to 1′ long) and erect. Petioles and rachis are polished red-brown, with a few dark narrow scales at the petiole base. The blade is 1-pinnate, the pinnae oblong to lanceolate, alternate with each other, with basal lobes overlapping the rachis, and with irregular round- or saw-toothed margins. The sori are in two diagonal rows, one on each side of the pinna midrib, and are covered by an elongate indusium.

Spleenworts are mostly small rock ferns growing in tight clumps from compact branching scaly rhizomes. The sori are elongate and diverging in parallel ranks between the leaflet midrib and margin, and with elongate indusia.

◆ **STATUS & HABITAT**—Frequent and wide ranging at low to mid elevations, growing on rocks and ledges, tree bases, or on rocky ground. This is the only spleenwort which regularly grows on the ground. When growing on rock substrates, and with other similar spleenworts, the paler green and dimorphic leaves help differentiate them.

BLACK-STEMMED SPLEENWORT

Asplenium resiliens

Spleenwort Family (*Aspleniaceae*)

Plants: 4"-8" tall (10-20 cm)

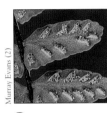

Similar to the ebony spleenwort except: leaves are not dimorphic, and are dark green and evergreen. Also, the petiole and rachis are black, the pinnae are shorter (ovate) and opposite in pairs on the rachis, with the basal lobe not overlapping the rachis. In addition, the sporangia have only 32 spores, indicating the plants are apogamous and do not undergo sexual fertilization in forming a new generation from the spores (see the section on the Fern Life Cycle). The ebony spleenwort has 64 spores per sporangium indicating that it does undergo sexual fertilization.

◆ **STATUS & HABITAT**—Uncommon in the Smokies. Black-stemmed spleenwort usually grows on limestone or other basic rocks and ledges at low elevations.

MAIDENHAIR SPLEENWORT

Murray Evans

*Asplenium
trichomanes ssp.
trichomanes*

Spleenwort Family
(*Aspleniaceae*)

Plants: 1½"-5" long
(4-13 cm)

Maidenhair spleenwort is similar to both the ebony and the black stemmed spleenworts, but it is much smaller, with all leaves alike. Maidenhair spleenwort leaves spread from a small rhizome tucked in crevices of acidic rocks and ledges. They are evergreen, narrow, and linear, ½" or less wide. The petiole and rachis are dark brown; the blade is 1-pinnate, the pinnae are opposite in pairs, oval to oblong, without basal lobes, and with rounded apex. Sori are elongate, but short and only up to 7 per pinna, with elongate indusia.

♦ **STATUS & HABITAT**—A plant of shaded, moist, acidic rocks and ledges. It is wide-ranging at low and mid elevations, occurring sporadically, and not commonly, but much more so than the black-stemmed spleenwort.

The other eastern U. S. subspecies, ssp. *quadrivalens*, prefers lime-stone or basic substrates, has twice as many chromosomes, and is more northeastern.

MOUNTAIN SPLEENWORT

Asplenium montanum

Spleenwort Family
(*Aspleniaceae*)

Leaves: 4"-7" long
(10-18 cm)

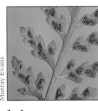

Murray Evans

Rebecca Shiflett

Mountain spleenwort is a small evergreen plant with leaves spreading or drooping from compact rhizome tufts in crevices of ledges and cliffs. Its leaves are up to 2" wide, but often smaller. The petiole is half the length of the blade, purple-brown at base, and green above. The rachis is green and flattened with a very narrow wing. The leaf blade is deltoid-lanceolate, pinnate-pinnatifid to 2-pinnate, reduced to a lobed apex of 4-7 pairs of subopposite pinnae. The margins are coarsely incised. Sori are few, (2-4) per segment, of varying lengths following the diverging veins of the segments.

◆ **STATUS & HABITAT**—This and the ebony spleenwort are our two most common spleenworts. Mountain spleenworts are wide-ranging at mid to high elevations on shaded, moist, acidic cliffs and ledges.

Lobed Spleenwort

*Asplenium
pinnatifidum*

Spleenwort Family
(*Aspleniaceae*)

Leaves: 4"-7" long
(10-18 cm)

Murray Evans (2)

Lobed spleenworts are small plants with small rhizomes tucked into rock crevices, obscured by old and current leaf bases. Its leaves are evergreen, arching or flattened against the rock substrate, and are not dimorphic. The petiole is shorter than the blade, lustrous red brown at the base becoming green above; the rachis is green. The blade is lanceolate, broadest at the base, deeply round-lobed at the base becoming less so toward the sharp pointed or tail-like apex. There are one to a few sori per lobe, following divergent free veins, and with indusia.

♦ **STATUS & HABITAT**—Rare in the Smokies; more common on sandstones of the Cumberland Plateau. Low elevations. Plants of shaded or exposed ledges and cliff faces, usually on sandstone, but also on other acidic rock.

The lobed spleenwort has an interesting evolutionary origin, characteristic of many ferns. It originated as sterile hybrids between the walking fern and the mountain spleenwort in which the chromosomes of some individuals somehow doubled, thereby becoming fertile plants.

WALL-RUE SPLEENWORT

*Asplenium
ruta-muraria*

Spleenwort Family
(*Aspleniaceae*)

Leaves: 4″-7″ long
(10-18 cm)

Rebecca Shiflett

This plant is similar to the mountain spleenwort. They are both of similar size and aspect; the leaf blade of both are quite similar. They differ in that the wall-rue grows on limestone; the mountain spleenwort on acidic granites and sandstones. Both are evergreen, but the wall-rue is light green and usually thin textured; the mountain spleenwort is dark green and more leathery. They are both 2-pinnate, with only a few pairs of lateral pinnae (only 2-4 pairs in the wall-rue), and becoming merely lobed at the leaf apex. The ultimate segments of the wall-rue are rhombic or narrowly fan-shaped with small saw teeth across the end. The ultimate segments of the Mountain spleenwort are narrow and oblong with irregular lobes.

◆ **STATUS & HABITAT**—Rare, at low elevations, on shaded limestone ledges and crevices. The mountain spleenwort is the common spleenwort of this pair in the Smokies, so the wall-rue would be a special find in a special place.

SENSITIVE FERN

Onoclea sensibilis

Wood Fern Family
(*Dryopteridaceae*)

Leaves: 1'-2' tall
(30-60 cm)

Murray Evans

Gerald Tang

Sensitive ferns are of moderate size; the coarse rhizome is long-creeping, branching, and scaly at the apex. The deciduous leaves are dimorphic, the axes with a few lanceolate scales. The vegetative leaf petiole is 1-1½ times the length of the blade, which is deltoid. The rachis is winged, joining to each other the opposite pinnae (which are lanceolate) with undulate to shallowly lobed margins. The fertile leaves are much reduced, but taller, narrower, and 2-pinnate. The leathery pinna lobes are tightly rolled around the sori, becoming bead-like, green when young, becoming purplish black, then becoming brown after the spores are shed. They persist usually into the following growing season.

◆ **STATUS & HABITAT**—Plants of swamps, marshes, or wet fields at low elevations, in large but only sporadic populations. The vegetative leaves resemble the netted chain fern, but the pinnae of the latter are mostly alternate, and the fertile leaves are very different.

*Diplazium
pycnocarpon*

Wood Fern Family
(*Dryopteridaceae*)

Leaves: 2'-3½' tall
(0.6-1.06 meters)

Murray Evans (2)

Glade fern leaves are 5"-9" wide, deciduous, and spaced along underground, long-creeping, scaly, blackish rhizomes. The leaf blade is lanceolate and pinnate, with numerous lanceolate pinnae which are tapered at the apex, and rounded at the base; without hairs or scales. The fertile leaves appear in the summer after the vegetative leaves and are taller, narrower, and with narrower pinnae. They are also more erect than the arching vegetative leaves. The sori are numerous in two divergent ranks the length of the pinnae, each about ⅛" long with the indusium arching over the sorus.

◆ **STATUS & HABITAT**—Sporadic and infrequent at low to mid elevations in rich wet bottomland woods and rocky seepage slopes.

   This species has a rich history of presumed hereditary relationships, and has historically been placed in *Homalosorus*, *Athyrium*, and *Asplenium*. It is now considered the single temperate eastern and midwestern North American relative of the large tropical genus *Diplazium*.

SILVERY GLADE FERN

Deparia acrostichoides

Wood Fern Family (*Dryopteridaceae*)

Leaves: 1¼'-3' tall (0.4-0.9 meter)

Rebecca Schillert (2)

Silvery glade fern leaves are deciduous and clumped irregularly along short-creeping rhizomes (which are covered with old petiole bases). The leaves are covered throughout with silvery, stiff hairs. The green petiole is shorter than the blade and displays blackish, crinkled, narrow scales mostly toward the dark brown petiole base. The leaf blade is regularly pinnate-pinnatifid, the pinna lobes have scalloped toothed margins. The elongate sori of fertile leaves diverge regularly in two ranks from the midrib to the margin of the lobes, each with a smooth elongate indusium. The fertile leaves appear later than the arching vegetative leaves and are somewhat narrower, taller, and more erect.

◆ **STATUS & HABITAT**—Common and wide ranging in wet soils of rich woods, stream banks, marshes, and seeps. It is a common and characteristic part of the stream-side flora of the rich deciduous forest.

In many identification manuals, this fern is *Athyrium thelypteroides*. As with the previous glade fern, it fits better with a large group of African and Asian *Deparia* relatives.

Athyrium filix-femina var. asplenioides

Wood Fern Family
(*Dryopteridaceae*)

Leaves: 1½'-3' tall
(0.45-0.9 meter)

Murray Evans (2)

This fern's leaves are deciduous, spreading to erect, 5"-14" wide, and are clustered at the apex of coarse ascending black rhizomes covered with old petiole bases. The petioles are as long as the blade, translucent reddish or light green in color with dark brown or black swollen bases, and with scattered brown crinkled scales. The leaf blades are ovate, widest at the second pinna pair from the blade base, 2-pinnate to 3-pinnate. The pinnae are ovate-lanceolate. The pinnules are about the same length above and below the pinna midrib, (especially note the lowest pinna pair), and become shorter toward the rachis. Sori are somewhat various, elongate, curved or hooked over the vein, or sometimes round. The indusium conforms to the sorus shape and has a hairy margin.

◆ **STATUS & HABITAT**—Common everywhere the soils are rich and moist.

This is often confused with the intermediate wood fern, which has a similar leaf appearance, but the latter is evergreen, the pinnules, especially of the basal pinna pair, are longer toward the rachis, and are much longer on the lower side than the upper side of the pinna midrib.

BLUNT-LOBED CLIFF FERN

Woodsia obtusa

Wood Fern Family
(*Dryopteridaceae*)

Leaves: 8″-2′ tall
(20-61 cm)

Murray Evans (2)

This is a modest-sized rock fern. Its leaves are clustered, its rhizome erect, clumped, obscured by old and current petiole bases, and with brown scales with a dark median stripe. Its leaves are 1½″-3½″ wide; the petiole is half the length of the blade, green to straw-colored, with pale brown scales, but without hairs. The blade is 2-pinnate, lanceolate, light green. The rachis has glandular hairs and scales; the pinnae nearly opposite. The segments are round tipped with toothed margins. The fertile leaves are erect and longer than the spreading arching vegetative leaves. The sori are round. The indusium is composed of several strap-like flaps attached under the sporangia, arching over them when young, and later pushed back and obscured by the maturing sporangia.

◆ **STATUS & HABITAT**—Plants of ledges, masonry walls, and rocky slopes, mostly on limestone. It is uncommon in the Smokies, found only in widely scattered small populations at low elevations.

There are two other smaller cliff ferns in the southern Appalachians, the rusty cliff fern (*Woodsia ilvensis*) and the mountain cliff fern (*Woodsia scopulina*), but neither are known in the Smokies.

CHRISTMAS FERN

Polystichum acrostichoides

Wood Fern Family
(*Dryopteridaceae*)

Leaves: 1'-2' long
(30-61 cm)

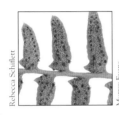

Christmas ferns have very scaly leaves arising from short, stocky, erect rhizomes covered with old petiole bases and light brown scales. The leaves are evergreen, dark green, and somewhat dimorphic. The vegetative leaves are more arching and shorter. The fertile leaves are taller, more erect, with the fertile pinnae constricted, more widely spaced apart, and confined to the leaf apex. When the spores are shed, this apical portion turns brown and withers. The petiole is one-third the length of the blade, densely scaly with light brown broad scales.

The blade is 1-pinnate, narrowly lanceolate. The rachis is scaly like the petiole. The pinnae are lanceolate with a prominent basal lobe (auricle), the margins are sharply toothed, each tooth apex with a stiff hair. The sori nearly cover the underside of the fertile pinna, and are individually round.

◆ **STATUS & HABITAT**—Abundant throughout the park. Found on shaded rocky slopes, mixed woods, boulder fields. Probably our most common and easily recognized fern. There are many named varieties and forms for this species based on peculiar and conspicuous leaf variations, but none are considered important taxonomically.

LOWLAND BRITTLE FERN

Cystopteris protrusa

Wood Fern Family
(*Dryopteridaceae*)

Leaves: 4"-16" tall
(10-41 cm)

Murray Evans (2)

This is a small deciduous fern with delicate light green leaves often growing in large patches. The leaves are in loose clumps on short-creeping, branching, underground rhizomes, the apex of which protrudes beyond the leaves (hence the Latin name). Fleshy green starch storage structures resembling short petiole bases are mixed with the petioles along the rhizome. The leaves have petioles as long as the blade, green with a dark base, and sparsely scaly at the base. The leaf blade is deltoid to ovate, 1½"-4½" wide, 2-pinnate at blade base. The pinnae are without hairs or scales, the ultimate segments toothed and/or lobed, the ultimate veinlets directed into the teeth. The sori are round and small; the indusium delicate, ovate, or pocket-shaped, without glandular hairs.

   This is one of the first deciduous ferns to appear in the spring; the first leaves are small, delicate, and only vegetative; successive leaves are taller, more robust, and fertile. First leaves may be only a few inches tall. Midsummer produced leaves may be 12" to 16" tall.

◆ **STATUS & HABITAT**—Common in rich woods at low and mid elevations, primarily terrestrial, but sometimes on rocks and ledges.

BULBLET BLADDER FERN

Cystopteris bulbifera

Wood Fern Family
(*Dryopteridaceae*)

Leaf: blade 1'-3' long
(0.3-0.9 meter)

Murray Evans (2)

This fern grows on and around wet limestone ledges and outcrops. The rhizome is short-creeping with abundant brown scales at the apex. The leaves are closely spaced among many persistent petiole bases. They are variable in length, with pinkish to green petioles much shorter than the blade, and sparsely scaly at the base. The blade is 2-pinnate to 3-pinnate-pinnatifid, narrowly deltoid, and always widest at the base. It is either relatively short and with an acute apex, or wand-like and up to 3' long with a long tapering apex. The rachis and costa are covered with glandular hairs, and usually with a few conspicuous green fleshy bulblets on the underside. The ultimate veinlets of the pinnules end in notches between the teeth. The sori are small, round, and inconspicuous. The indusium is delicate, pocket-like, and covered with glandular hairs.

The bulblets drop to the ground and provide a means of vegetative reproduction.

♦ **STATUS & HABITAT**—Low elevations on shaded wet ledges and rocky slopes; rare because limestone habitat is limited in the Smokies.

MARGINAL WOOD FERN

Dryopteris marginalis

Wood Fern Family
(*Dryopteridaceae*)

Leaves: 6″-3′ tall
(15-91 cm)

Murray Evans

Rebecca Schiflett

Marginal wood fern leaves grow in a crown at the stocky, erect, rhizome apex. They surround a ring of tightly curled buds of next year's leaves. They are 4″-10″ wide, leathery, evergreen, dark blue-green. The petioles are one-quarter the length of the blade, densely scaly with red-brown concolorous scales. The blade is ovate, pinnate-pinnatifid to 2-pinnate at the base in more elaborate leaf forms. The pinnae are lanceolate, and the segment margins have rounded low teeth. Round sori with smooth reniform indusia are close to the leaf margins, hence the common and scientific names.

Wood ferns and shield ferns are generally moderate to large ferns with leaves in a crown or a tight clump around next year's scaly leaf buds. The sori are round in a horse-shoe shape (reniform), covered with an indusium of similar shape.

♦ **STATUS & HABITAT**—Common at low to mid elevations; rich woods, rocky slopes, and mossy crevices of boulders and ledges.

Dryopteris intermedia

Wood Fern Family
(*Dryopteridaceae*)

Leaves: 10"-3' tall
(25-91 cm)

Rebecca Schiflett (2)

This fern's evergreen leaves are in a crown at the apex of the erect, stocky, scaly, rhizome. Its leaves are dark green and 5"-10" wide. The leaf petiole is one-third the length of the blade and scaly with golden to red-brown scales. The blade is ovate, of firm texture, and 3-pinnate. The rachis and costa are glandular hairy. On the lowest pair of pinnae the pinnules are much longer on the lower side of the costa than above the costa. On the same pinna pair the innermost lower pinnule next to the rachis is shorter than the adjacent pinnule of the same pinna. The longest lower pinnules are only up to two times as long as the upper pinnules. The ultimate segment margins have small sharply pointed teeth, but without spines. The sori are equidistant between segment midvein and margin; the indusium is covered with glandular hairs.

Understanding the characteristics of the lowest pinna pair of the leaf and the distribution of leaf glandular hairs is key to distinguishing this from mountain wood fern and southern lady fern.

♦ **STATUS & HABITAT**—This is one of the most common ferns of the Smokies. It is wide ranging in rich woods, rocky slopes, mossy boulders and ledges, and wooded stream margins at all elevations.

MOUNTAIN WOOD FERN

Dryopteris campyloptera

Wood Fern Family
(*Dryopteridaceae*)

Leaves: 1½'-3' tall
(0.45-0.9 meter)

Rebecca Schiflett (2)

This is very similar to the intermediate wood fern. It differs, in our region, in growing only above 4,000' elevation (where they grow together). It is deciduous, not evergreen. It grows taller and broader (10"-18" wide) and has a softer leaf texture. The leaf dissection is the same. The glandular hairs do not occur on the rachis and costa, but may occur on the indusium. The architecture of the basal pinna pair differ; the innermost lower pinnules are longer than the adjacent pinnules. The longest lower pinnules are 3-4 times longer than the longest upper pinnules of the same lowermost pinna, and the lower pinnules are large enough that the stalk of the third lower pinnule away from the rachis is beyond the stalk of the fourth upper pinnule away from the rachis.

◆ **STATUS & HABITAT**—Common in high elevation rocky valleys, ridges and summits in rich soils.

This fern grows with the intermediate wood fern and the southern lady fern above 4,000', all three in abundance, and all three superficially similar. You may need to look closely at several leaves or plants to become satisfied with an identification.

Dryopteris goldiana

Wood Fern Family
(*Dryopteridaceae*)

Leaves: 1½'-3' tall
(0.45-0.9 meter)

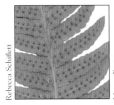

Goldie's fern is a large fern with firm leaves in a crown surrounding, or in an irregular clump among, stout, very scaly leaf buds at the apex of stout ascending rhizomes. It is deciduous and dark green; the scales of the rhizome and petiole are large and broad, with dark red-brown centers and paler margins. The scaly petiole is two-thirds the length of the blade. The blade is pinnate-pinnatifid, 1'-3' long, 8"-16" wide, ovate, then tapering abruptly to an acute apex. The lowest pinnae are only slightly shorter than the longest pinnae, and lanceolate in outline as the innermost pinna lobes are shorter than the middle lobes of the same pinna. The sori are in two rows closer to the lobe midrib than the lobe margin. The indusium is smooth and without glands.

◆ **STATUS & HABITAT**—Infrequent, at low to mid elevations. In wooded, rich, rocky seepage slopes, depressions, or margins of swamps. Although this fern is generally considered a swamp fern, it does occur on wooded mountainsides along water sources, particularly in the Big Creek area.

Log Fern

Dryopteris celsa

Wood Fern Family
(*Dryopteridaceae*)

Leaves: 1½'-3' tall
(0.45-0.9 meter)

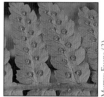

Murray Evans (2)

This is a large deciduous fern with firm leaves in a compact row among a cluster of scaly leaf buds at the apex of stout creeping rhizomes. The petiole is one-third the length of blade, scaly with broad light to dark brown scales, many with a darker brown median stripe. The blade is broadly lanceolate, 15"-30" long, 7"-12" wide, pinnate-pinnatifid, and gradually, not abruptly, tapered at the apex. The basal pinnae are two-thirds to three-quarters the length of the longest pinnae. The innermost pinna lobes adjacent to the rachis are as long as the median lobes of the same pinna. The margins have broad, low, flattened teeth. The sori are in two rows, each less than half way from the midrib to the margin. The indusium is smooth and without glands.

◆ **STATUS & HABITAT**—Rare, known only in a few low elevation sites. Found in swamp woods or along rocky stream beds.

The log fern is very similar to Goldie's fern. It is considered to be derived from hybridization between *Dryopteris goldiana* and the southeastern coastal plain species, *Dryopteris ludoviciana*.

CRESTED WOOD FERN

Dryopteris cristata

Wood Fern Family
(*Dryopteridaceae*)

Leaves: 14″-2′ tall
(36-61 cm)

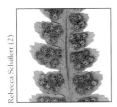

Rebecca Schiffert (2)

Crested wood fern displays partially evergreen dimorphic leaves arising in a cluster at the apex of compact horizontal rhizomes. The rhizome and petiole scales are pale red-brown and concolorous. The dimorphic leaves are pale green; the vegetative leaves are short, lanceolate, arching, and evergreen. The fertile leaves are taller, erect, narrowly lanceolate, and deciduous. The more conspicuous, stiffly erect fertile leaf blades are 10″-20″ long, 3″-6″ wide, and pinnate-pinnatifid. The pinna are deeply lobed and toothed. Fertile pinnae are confined to the upper half of the blade and are often turned nearly horizontal to the ground, like a venetian blind. The basal pinnae are triangular and only half as long as the middle pinnae. The sori are in two rows half way between the midvein and the margins. The indusium is without glandular hairs.

◆ **STATUS & HABITAT**—Rare in the Smokies, more frequent but still widely scattered in surrounding areas. Found in low elevation swamps, bogs, and marshes.

It is occasionally possible to find *Dryopteris* hybrids. They almost always grow with the parents and display intermediate characteristics.

APPALACHIAN ROCK POLYPODY

Polypodium appalachianum

Polypody Family
(*Polypodiaceae*)

Leaves: 3″-1′ tall
(8-30 cm)

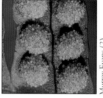

Murray Evans (2)

This fern's leaves are dark green, evergreen, leathery, 1″-3″ wide, and pinnatifid. The lateral lobes are broadly attached to the rachis. The leaves are spaced along the exposed creeping, branching rhizome. The rhizome is densely covered with ovate-lanceolate, light brown scales. The petiole is two-thirds the length of the blade. The blade is narrowly deltoid-lanceolate, widest at or near the base, with widely scattered, inconspicuous, small golden-brown scales. The leaf lobes taper to a rounded acute apex, the margins are smooth and shallowly undulate. The sori are large and round, slightly indented into the leaf tissue and without indusia. Mixed among the sporangia are many minute glassy clubs (sporangiasters), the rounded ends of which are covered with blunt spines. There are usually over 40 sporangiasters per sori.

This is an easily recognizable fern with its exposed scaly rhizome, simple architecture, and large golden-colored sori. It is not necessary to struggle over "sporangiasters" unless one is trying to differentiate it from *Polypodium virginianum*, which is not found in the Smokies.

◆ **STATUS & HABITAT**—Frequent and wide ranging. Found on boulders, ledges, and sometimes on exposed tree roots or trunks.

Pleopeltis
polypodioides
var.michauxiana

Polypody Family
(*Polypodiaceae*)

Leaves: 2″-6″ tall (5-15 cm)

Resurrection fern is similar to the Appalachian rock polypody except rhizomes and leaves are only about half as big, in length and width. Also, the rhizome, petiole, and lower surface of the leaf blades are all densely covered with gray scales with pale margins, thus making the plants look gray-green. The lobes of the pinnatifid blade are rounded at the apex, the sori are submarginal on the lobes, without indusia. The leaf scales around the sorus partially cover the sorus.

The resurrection fern is placed in *Polypodium* in many of our regional fern manuals. It is now placed in *Pleopeltis* which is a tropical similarly scaly genus of polypody.

◆ **STATUS & HABITAT**—Found infrequently at low elevations. Grows on tree trunks and limbs, and also on rocks. During dry periods the leaves curl up, which reduces surface area and evaporation, and will uncurl when moisture is again available; hence the common name.

Generally, Polypodies grow on either rocks or trees. Most of them are tropical, and, north of Florida, there are only the two genera discussed here.

INDEPENDENT FERN GAMETOPHYTES IN THE SMOKIES

When fern gametophytes are found "in the wild," they are generally considered simply part of the normal fern life cycle of alternating tiny independent haploid gametophytes bearing sex organs with sex cells (sperm and eggs) and much larger diploid sporophyte plants producing spores (see section on Fern Life Cycle).

However, there are three fern species in the Smokies that are known only as gametophytes, which almost never produce sex organs, but regularly produce gemmae which allow them to reproduce more gametophytes vegetatively in the absence of sexual reproduction. These are mostly tropical ferns, and it is generally accepted that climate conditions at some time in the past caused the sporophyte part of the life cycle to became extinct but not the gametophyte generation. Much of this study is primarily by Dr. Donald Farrar of Iowa State University and various colleagues.

In order to find and identify these organisms, fern fanciers have to think and act like bryologists—students of mosses and liverworts. A hand lens is essential, and also a more powerful dissecting scope or compound microscope is useful (collecting is prohibited in the park without a permit). The plants are flat, one cell thick, branching filamentous ribbons, measured in millimeters, forming delicate pale green mats on moist dark crevices and ledges, mostly in cave-like overhanging rock formations.

One is a shoestring fern (*Vittaria* in the family Vittariaceae), the other two are filmy ferns in the Hymenophyllaceae Family, one *Hymenophyllum* and one *Trichomanes*.

For a more complete discussion of these plants than the following, refer to the 1993 *Flora of North America, Vol. 2*, cited in the bibliography.

*Vittaria
appalachiana*

Shoestring Fern Family
(*Vittariaceae*)

Plant: ⅛" tall
(3 mm)

Don Farrar (2)

This gametophyte of the tropical genus *Vittaria* occurs on continuously damp and shaded crevices, ledges, and cave openings, on sandstone and other acidic rock formations. It is ribbon-like and irregularly lobed, one cell thick, and up to ⅛" high. It reproduces vegetatively by fragmentation of the ribbons and from detachable spindle-shaped filaments one cell wide and up to 12 cells long borne on short stalks at the apex of some lobes. It can make extensive mats and covers boulders and crevice walls under the right conditions.

◆ **STATUS & HABITAT**—Although more common on the Cumberland Plateau to the west, it is known from several places at low and mid elevations in the Smokies. It is the most commonly found of the three independent gametophytes. It ranges from Alabama and South Carolina northeast along the Appalachians to Ohio, Maryland, and Pennsylvania. It is similar to, but not identical with, the gametophytes found associated with *Vittaria lineata*, a shoestring fern of south Florida and the New World tropics.

TAYLOR'S FILMY FERN

Hymenophyllum tayloriae

Filmy Fern Family
(*Hymenophyllaceae*)

Plant: ⅛" tall
(3 mm)

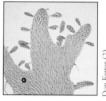

Don Farrar (2)

Like the *Vittaria*, this gametophyte is also nearly microscopic, irregularly lobed, and ribbon-like. It is one cell thick and only several cells wide. The gemmae are more scattered along the margins of the lobes and are paddle-shaped and more than one cell wide across the middle. It also reproduces vegetatively, either by fragmentation or by detachment of the gemmae.

Currently known from northwest Alabama, and a few counties where North Carolina, South Carolina, and Georgia adjoin. It has recently been found in the Smokies, and reported by Dr. Paul Davison of the University of North Alabama.

◆ **STATUS & HABITAT**—It can occur in permanently shaded and moist rock ledges along stream ravines and around waterfalls.

There have been a few sightings of very small juvenile sporophyte plants of this species with leaves less than ⅛" long. They were not mature, had no spores, but had distinctive characteristics of *Hymenophyllum*.

Trichomanes intricatum

Filmy Fern Family
(*Hymenophyllaceae*)

Plant: ⅛″ tall
(3 mm)

Don Farrar (2)

This gametophyte resembles little patches of stiff green cotton or felt tucked into dark rock crevices. It consists of irregularly branched strings of cells, one cell wide and many cells long. They resemble small filamentous green algae, and do not resemble the other two gametophyte fern species in this book. Gemmae are simply short strings of unspecialized cells capable of breaking off the main branches and growing a new mass.

◆ **STATUS & HABITAT**—Grows in dark, humid rock crevices, under overhangs or in shallow caves, at low to mid elevations. This is the most wide-spread of the three independent gametophyes and occurs from northern Alabama up the Appalachians to New Hampshire and Vermont and west to Illinois. In part of its range it overlaps with two other *Trichomanes* species which exhibit the conventional sporophyte-gametophyte fern life cycle. The gametophytes of these two (*Trichomanes petersii* and *T. boschianum*) can also be found independent of their sporophytes.

BIBLIOGRAPHY

Editorial Committee. *Flora of North America, Vol. 2: Pteridophytes and Gymnosperms*. 1993. Oxford Univ. Press: New York. A comprehensive technical manual to the flora of North America.

Evans, A. Murray; Pteridophyte Families; in Wofford, B. Eugene. *Guide to the Vascular Plants of the Blue Ridge*. 1989. Univ. of Georgia Press: Athens. A comprehensive student manual to the flora of the Blue Ridge Mts. of VA, TN, NC and GA, with keys to all species, notes about their distribution, but no overall descriptions or illustrations.

Hallowell, Anne C. and Barbara G. *Fern Finder: A Guide to Native Ferns of Northeastern and Central North America*. 1981. Nature Study Guild: Rochester, NY. A quick and easy pocket-sized starter guide with thorough keys and line drawings to all the ferns in our area, but none of the fern allies. A good companion to any fern flora manual.

Lellinger, David B. *A Field Manual of the Ferns and Fern-allies of the United States and Canada*. 1985. Smithsonian Institution Press: Washington. A comprehensive photographically illustrated user-friendly manual to the pteridophytes of North America, north of Mexico, with useful chapters concerning fern biosystematics and evolution.

ILLUSTRATED GLOSSARY

Parts of a fern

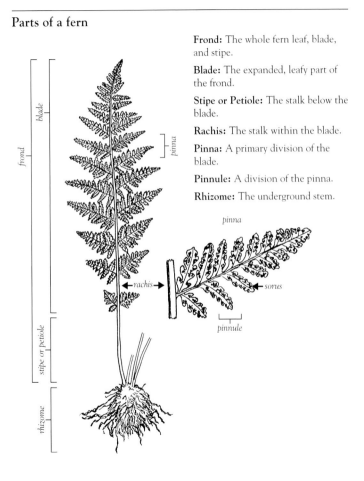

Frond: The whole fern leaf, blade, and stipe.

Blade: The expanded, leafy part of the frond.

Stipe or Petiole: The stalk below the blade.

Rachis: The stalk within the blade.

Pinna: A primary division of the blade.

Pinnule: A division of the pinna.

Rhizome: The underground stem.

Degrees of frond dissection

Undivided

no pinnae

Once-divided

*pinna connected
at base*

*pinna separate
at base*

Twice-divided

pinna divided

Thrice-divided

pinnules divided

Pinna and pinnule margins

Smooth

Toothed

Lobed

Sorus patterns

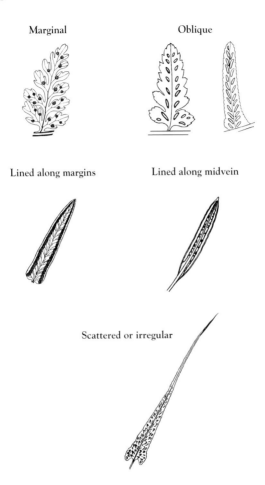

Marginal

Oblique

Lined along margins

Lined along midvein

Scattered or irregular

GLOSSARY

ALLOTETRAPLOID. Species which, in the course of evolution, formed from the hybridization of individuals of two different diploid species, then doubled its chromosomes, which then allows sexual fertilization.

ANGIOSPERMS. Flowering plants. Seed plants, in which the seed is enclosed within the ovary of a flower. See Gymnosperms.

ANNULUS. A row or patch of specialized cells in the fern sporangium wall, which, upon shrinking, causes the sporangium to open and release the mature spores.

APOGAMY (APOGAMOUS). Literally, without gametes. A form of vegetative reproduction that mimics sexual reproduction. In the pteridophytes, meiosis does not occur in the sporangium, so the chromosome number is not reduced by half; the spores germinate to produce gametophytes, but sexual reproduction does not occur on the gametophyte, and a juvenile sporophyte simply buds from the gametophyte. See Vegetative Reproduction.

AREOLAE (AREOLATE). Describing a leaf venation pattern, in which the areolae are defined by a surrounding network of veins.

AXIS (PL. AXES). In reference to fern leaf architecture, the stem-like portions of the leaf blade on which the laminar segments are borne.

BICOLOR (BICOLOROUS). In reference to leaf scales of two colors, usually with a darker central stripe, or a darker margin.

BLADE. Leaves are mostly composed of a petiole, or stipe (the basal stalk-like portion) and the blade (the flattened laminar portion). In a compound leaf, the blade is all the leaflets and adjoining axes taken together.

CIRCUMBOREAL. Growing within the band surrounding the northern hemisphere, lying between the warmer temperate zone and the colder arctic or polar zone.

CONCOLOR (CONCOLOROUS). Of one color; refer to Bicolor.

COSTA. The primary axis of a pinna of a compound leaf. Compare with midvein, costule, and rachis.

COSTULE. The secondary axis of a pinna; joining the pinnule to the costa.

DECIDUOUS. A growth strategy in which the annual foliage dies back to the perennial rhizome over winter.

DELTOID. Triangular in shape, usually as in undivided leaf blades, or segments of leaf blades, or defining the outline of compound leaf blades.

DIMORPHIC. Having two different forms; usually referring to fertile and sterile (with vegetative tissue, but without reproductive structures) leaves or portions of leaves.

DIPLOID. Plant cells with two sets of chromosomes. See Tetraploid and Allotetraploid.

EVERGREEN. Plants having green leaves throughout the year, or, at least, green leaves overwintering until a new leaf set appears in the spring.

EXTIRPATED. An organism that has been eliminated, intentionally or accidentally, from a known locality, or all, or part, of its known range.

GEMMA (PL. GEMMAE). A particular vegetative reproductive structure, which, when dropped to the ground from its parent plant, can grow into a new plant without participating in sexual reproduction.

GLABROUS. Plant stems and leaves without scales, hairs or glands.

GLAND. An epidermal unicellular or multicellular structure containing or secreting waxes, resins or sugars.

GLANDULAR HAIR. A hair with a spherical gland at its apex. See Gland.

GYMNOSPERMS. Woody vascular plants bearing naked seeds on woody cone scales in cones, as opposed to angiosperms which bear seeds enclosed in ovaries in the female part of the flower. Familiar gymnosperms are pine, red cedar, white cedar, spruce, redwood, bald cypress, larch, etc.

HAIRS. Epidermal appendages composed of a single file of few to many cells.

HERBACEOUS. Composed of soft tissue without woody secondary growth, as found in stems and branches of shrubs and trees.

INDUMENT. A collective term for the presence of hairs, scales, or glands.

INDUSIUM. A thin scale-like membrane partially or completely covering the young sporangia in the sori of many ferns; usually pushed aside as the sporangia enlarge and mature. A true indusium is a de novo structure arising from epidermal cells of the leaf adjacent to the sorus; a false indusium is a folded- or rolled-under leaf margin covering sori borne along the leaf margin of certain fern groups.

JOINTED. With reference to Equisetum, the horsetails and scouring Rushes, the stems and branches have regular weak joints which are easily pulled apart.

LAMINA. The flattened, expanded part or parts of a leaf blade.

LANCEOLATE. Elongate and narrow shape; lance-like, broadest below the middle and tapering to the apex.

MIDVEIN. The central vein of an undivided leaf or of a leaf segment. See also: Rachis, Costa.

OBLONG. Longer than wide, with the sides more or less parallel and the base and apex rounded.

OVATE. Broadly rounded at the base, narrowing above, becoming more or less pointed at the apex.

PALMATE. More than three parts, lobed, divided or branched from a single point; palm- or hand-like.

PERENNIAL. An expected life span of more than two, to many, years.

PETIOLE. The "stalk" of a leaf which attaches to the stem and carries the leaf blade. See also Stipe.

PINNA (PL. PINNAE). The primary division, or leaflet, of a pinnately, or more divided, compound leaf, either constricted at its attachment to the rachis (sessile), or stalked then with a costa.

PINNATE. Describes a compound leaf with two rows of undivided pinna, one on each side of the axis, or rachis, of the blade.

PINNATIFID. In reference to the outline of a leaf blade or pinna which is deeply lobed or incised to the midrib, but in which the segment is not constricted at its base. See Pinna and Pinnate.

PINNULE. On a compound leaf, the next order of division of the pinna, the pinnule is constricted or stalked at its point of attachment to the axis of the pinna (the costa).

RACHIS. The primary axis of a compound leaf blade.

REFUGIUM. A place of refuge; a geographic location in which biological organisms have been thought to have retreated and survived during hard times and from which they could spread and repopulate a larger area.

RENIFORM. Kidney-shaped; or

more curved to horseshoe-shaped, as in the indusium of many dryopteroid ferns.

RHIZOME. The stem of Pteridophytes; it is short or long, creeping, subterranean, or upon the ground, or climbing rock or tree surfaces. It is perennial and bears the roots and the leaves.

SCALES. Contrary to hairs, they are more than one cell, and usually many cells, wide. With hairs and glands they make up the indument of many plants.

SESSILE. An attachment of one part to another without an intervening stalk.

SORUS (PL. SORI). A cluster of sporangia usually with a distinctive shape; it may be covered by an indusium, or it may include distinctive glandular hairs (sporangiasters) mixed with the sporangia.

SPECIATION. The process of forming new species from existing gene pools in the course of evolution.

SPORANGIUM (PL. SPORANGIA). The principal structures in the sorus; they produce the spores. In the majority of ferns, each sporangium produces about 64 spores; but in some groups, such as *Botrychium*, *Ophioglossum*, *Osmunda* and the fern allies many more spores are produced in each sporangium.

SPOROPHYLL. A fertile leaf, bearing sporangia. It usually also has, but may lack, green photosynthetic leaf tissue. Leaves not bearing sporangia can be designated vegetative leaves or trophophylls.

STIPE. The "stalk" of the leaf joining the blade to the stem, or rhizome. Stipe is a term specific to Pteridophytes; "petiole" can be applied to all vascular plant leaves.

STOMATES. Submicroscopic openings in the epidermis of leaves, and some stems, through which gas exchange occurs between the interior tissues of the plant and the exterior atmosphere. Using magnification, they can be recognized by the two kidney bean shaped cells, one on each side of the opening.

STROBILUS (PL. STROBILI). A distinctive elongate cluster of scale-like leaves each with one, or a few, sporangia, generally terminal on a few branches of the Fern Allies. They superficially resemble tiny spruce or fir cones.

TETRAPLOID. Organisms that, in the course of evolution, have doubled the expected diploid number of chromosomes. See

Allotetraploid.

TROPHOPHYLL. See
Sporophyll.

ULTIMATE. In the sense of
describing Pteridophytes, the
final or last division, or forking.

VASCULAR BUNDLES. The
specialized elongate bundles of
cellular tubes that conduct water
and dissolved metabolic materials
throughout the roots, stems, and
leaves of pteridophytes and other
vascular plants.

VEGETATIVE PROPAGA-
TION. The production of new
individuals of a species without
sexual fertilization. See Gemma.

VELUM. With reference to
Isoetes (quillworts), the eyelid-
like partial covering over the
cavity in the flattened leaf base
in which the sporangium is
borne.

Species Index
Common and scientific names